P9-DTP-322

*On Springer Mountain, in Georgia, a bronze plaque
marks the southern terminus of the Appalachian Trail.*

HARDCOVER STAMP: ADAPTED FROM THE BRONZE PLAQUE ABOVE.

MOUNTAIN ADVENTURE

Exploring the Appalachian Trail

By Ron Fisher

Photographed by Sam Abell

Prepared by the Special Publications Division
National Geographic Society, Washington, D.C.

MOUNTAIN ADVENTURE
Exploring the Appalachian Trail

By RON FISHER
Photographed by SAM ABELL
Illustrations by ALAN SINGER

Published by THE NATIONAL GEOGRAPHIC SOCIETY
GILBERT M. GROSVENOR, *President and*
Chairman of the Board
MELVIN M. PAYNE, THOMAS W. MCKNEW,
Chairmen Emeritus
OWEN R. ANDERSON, *Executive Vice President*
ROBERT L. BREEDEN, *Senior Vice President,*
Publications and Educational Media

Prepared by THE SPECIAL PUBLICATIONS DIVISION
DONALD J. CRUMP, *Director*
PHILIP B. SILCOTT, *Associate Director*
BONNIE S. LAWRENCE, *Assistant Director*

Staff for this Book
MARTHA C. CHRISTIAN, *Managing Editor*
THOMAS B. POWELL III, *Illustrations Editor*
VIVIANE Y. SILVERMAN, *Art Director*
VICTORIA COOPER, DIANA L. VANEK, *Researchers*
STEPHEN J. HUBBARD, *Research Assistant*
RICHARD M. CRUM, RON FISHER, H. ROBERT MORRISON,
THOMAS J. O'NEILL, *Picture Legend Writers*
JUDITH F. BELL, *Map Editor*
GARY M. JOHNSON, *Map Production Coordinator*
SANDRA F. LOTTERMAN, *Editorial Assistant*
ARTEMIS S. LAMPATHAKIS, *Illustrations Assistant*
MARISA J. FARABELLI, *Art Secretary*

Engraving, Printing, and Product Manufacture
GEORGE V. WHITE, *Director, Manufacturing and*
Quality Management
VINCENT P. RYAN, *Manager, Manufacturing and*
Quality Management
DAVID V. SHOWERS, *Production Manager*
KEVIN P. HEUBUSCH, *Production Project Manager*
LEWIS R. BASSFORD, *Assistant Production Manager*
KATHLEEN M. CIRUCCI, TIMOTHY H. EWING,
Senior Production Assistants
CAROL R. CURTIS, *Senior Production Staff Assistant*
SUSAN A. BENDER, CATHERINE G. CRUZ, KAREN KATZ,
LISA A. LAFURIA, ELIZA MORTON, DRU STANCAMPIANO,
Staff Assistants
DIANNE L. HARDY, *Indexer*

Copyright © 1988 National Geographic Society.
All rights reserved. Reproduction of the whole or any part
of the contents without written permission is prohibited.

Library of Congress CIP Data: page 196.

Seeking fellowship with the wilderness, a
hiker descends the white-blazed
Appalachian Trail on Blood Mountain, in
Georgia. PRECEDING PAGES: *Fallen birch*
passes trail-like through a bed of ferns.

Contents

*Winding through the Appalachians from
Springer Mountain, in Georgia,
to Katahdin, in Maine, the 2,100-mile
Appalachian National Scenic Trail passes
through 14 states. This long-distance
hiking trail, part of the National
Trails System, is within a day's drive of nearly
two-thirds of the U.S. population.*

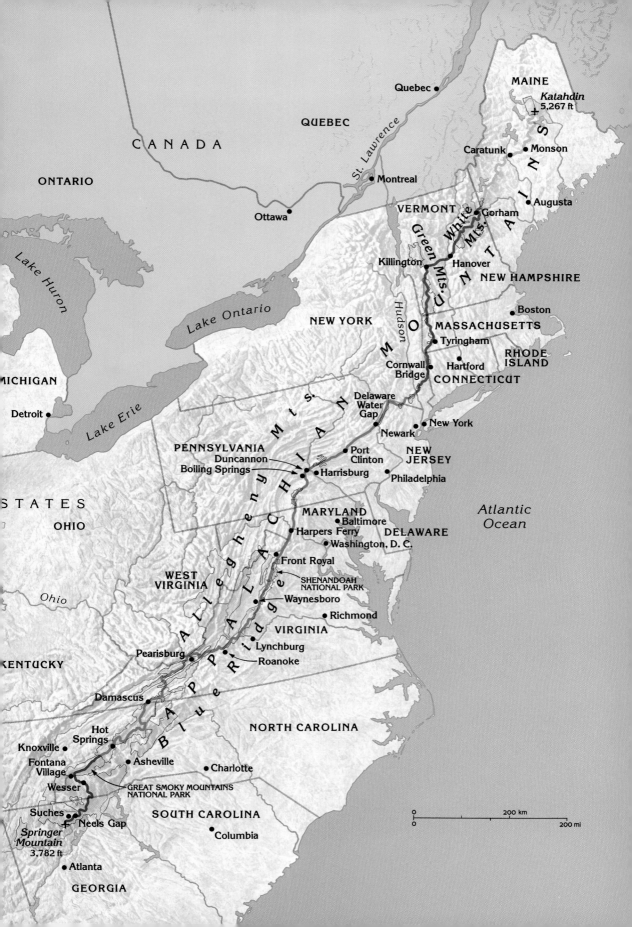

CANADA

ONTARIO

QUEBEC

St. Lawrence

Quebec

MAINE

Katahdin
5,267 ft

Monson

Caratunk

Augusta

Ottawa

Montreal

VERMONT

Gorham

Green Mts.

White Mts.

MOUNTAINS

NEW HAMPSHIRE

Killington

Hanover

Boston

MASSACHUSETTS

NEW YORK

Hudson

Tyringham

RHODE
ISLAND

Lake Ontario

Cornwall
Bridge

Hartford

CONNECTICUT

Lake Huron

MICHIGAN

Detroit

Lake Erie

Delaware
Water
Gap

Newark

New York

PENNSYLVANIA

Allegheny Mts.

Port
Clinton

NEW
JERSEY

STATES

OHIO

Duncannon

Boiling Springs

Harrisburg

Philadelphia

Ohio

MARYLAND

Baltimore

Harpers Ferry

Washington, D. C.

DELAWARE

*Atlantic
Ocean*

WEST
VIRGINIA

APPALACHIAN

Front Royal

SHENANDOAH
NATIONAL PARK

Waynesboro

Richmond

VIRGINIA

Lynchburg

KENTUCKY

Pearisburg

Blue Ridge

Roanoke

Damascus

NORTH CAROLINA

Hot
Springs

Knoxville

Asheville

Charlotte

Fontana
Village

Wesser

GREAT SMOKY MOUNTAINS
NATIONAL PARK

SOUTH CAROLINA

Suches

Neels Gap

Columbia

*Springer
Mountain*
3,782 ft

Atlanta

GEORGIA

0   200 km
0   200 mi

Yesterday's Vision, Today's Trail

From a union of vision and energy the Appalachian Trail was born. The dream of a wilderness footpath that would stretch the length of the Appalachians from Georgia to Maine originated with Benton MacKaye. That dream, which fired the imaginations of many and quickly won support, ultimately was carried to reality largely through the indefatigable efforts of Myron Avery. In many ways these two talented individuals were much alike. Both were New Englanders, both were Harvard graduates, and both had careers in the federal government. Both men loved the natural world intensely and drew their personal strength from it. Yet, MacKaye was ever the dreamer, the planner, the philosopher; Avery was the hard-driving doer, the pragmatic idealist.

MacKaye first suggested an Appalachian trail in 1921 in an article published in the *Journal of the American Institute of Architects.* The time was ripe for such a proposal, and from that seed grew the beginnings of a trail movement based on a volunteer work ethic that is unparalleled in history. Avery first became involved with the idea in 1927, near the beginning of his quarter-century of leadership in the Appalachian Trail Conference. He quickly demonstrated an ability to inspire others to join in the trail construction movement. With infectious enthusiasm and phenomenal energy, Avery traveled the Appalachians organizing new groups of volunteers while spurring existing groups to lay out, build, and blaze new sections of trail and to maintain completed sections.

In 1937—a mere 16 years after MacKaye's original article—the Appalachian Trail was complete. Avery's hardy army of volunteers had turned MacKaye's visionary dream into a reality. The goal was accomplished—but not without a price. In 1935 a philosophical difference over the construction of skyline drives and their impact on the trail had led to a breach between

Myron Avery, pushing a measuring wheel, leads trail volunteers up Hunt Spur of Katahdin, in Maine. The first person to hike the entire A.T., Avery once said that his "measuring wheel triumphed over all obstacles ... but in all the ... miles of its travels, the Katahdin trails were its severest test."

Father of the Appalachian Trail, Benton MacKaye—regional planner, forester, and conservationist—envisioned the trail as part of a social experiment to make the world more habitable. Maritime attorney Myron Avery (right), measuring trail in the Great Smokies, was the doer who organized volunteers for the A.T. project. His efforts helped transform the dream into reality.

Avery and MacKaye that was never to be reconciled. But the trail itself continued to take shape through the commitment of individual volunteers— often termed the "soul" of the trail by MacKaye.

Today the trail requires sophisticated management programs in 14 states, involving multiple national parks, forests, and other federal jurisdictions; numerous state parks, forests, and game lands; and local parks and watershed lands. The tasks are monumental. They include the maintenance of not only the footpath and the shelters along it, but also the thousands of acres of protected corridor lands being acquired by the federal government. Yet, this management challenge is being well met by the volunteers—those committed individuals who love the trail and know it best. For this tradition to continue, however, the pool of volunteers must be self-renewing, springing from that well of idealism exemplified originally by MacKaye and Avery.

The soul of the trail remains strong, but the challenges to its physical body require constant vigilance. The isolated and scenic character of the A.T. will continue to be threatened as urban sprawl and second-home development approach in many places the very boundaries of the protected corridor. Hence, it is critical to complete the acquisition of a corridor of

FROM THE ARCHIVES OF THE APPALACHIAN TRAIL CONFERENCE (BOTH)

adequate width before the opportunity is permanently lost. If protected now, the A.T. can forever remain one of our nation's premier treasures and a memorial to the once formidable wilderness that presented such an obstacle to the early settlers as they pushed the nation's frontiers westward.

The Appalachian Trail holds many different values for different people—values that will only grow with the passage of time as undeveloped lands continue to be diminished. Celebrating the A.T.'s first 50 years, this book reveals the trail's essential nature and speaks of the deep commitment to its preservation on the part of so many Americans.

David M. Sherman

EDITOR'S NOTE: Dave Sherman, one of many in the army of A.T. volunteers, is a 2,000-miler who knows the trail and its history well. In addition to being active in the Appalachian Trail Conference and the Potomac Appalachian Trail Club, he is the father of the Benton MacKaye Trail, a 250-mile hiking trail now under construction from Springer Mountain to the Smokies. This is one of several long-distance loop trails connected to the A.T., conceived and built by the spiritual heirs of MacKaye and Avery.

The Southern Snows of Spring

It might as well be winter.

Though the calendar says early April, a freakish spring storm has dropped more than a foot of snow on the Southeast, and the Appalachians from Virginia well down into Georgia are buried beneath a frigid white blanket. Roadside cattle peer skyward, looking worried. Photographer Sam Abell and I, driving along a gravel road in Georgia, twist and climb upward through piney woods filled with snow. We stop at a trailhead, where a couple of other cars are already parked—one from North Carolina, the other from Virginia. As we get out and prepare to walk—donning wool socks and boots, stocking caps and mittens—clouds the color of bruises scud overhead, and the wind whistles in bare, leafless trees. It feels like Maine, not Georgia.

By midmorning, we're trudging toward the summit of Springer Mountain, southern terminus of the Appalachian Trail. In clusters of mountain laurel, snow slides off branches in the warming sun and hits the ground, *plop.* Water drips from trees swaying in the wind. No birds sing; no green leaves brighten the prospect. It's a hill of bare brown branches and white snow.

I'm reminded of a line from an old hymn sung in Appalachian churches. "There are blossoms of gladness 'Neath the winter's snow." I've been browsing lately in old hymnals and have been struck by the number of references to hills and valleys, to rocks and rivers. Many of the songs might have been written with hikers in mind.

We meet a couple, bundled against the cold, coming toward us down the mountain, Suzie and Jerry Gramling, of Virginia Beach, Virginia. They have just climbed part way up Springer with their son—another Jerry—who plans to walk all the way to Maine, a journey he expects will take him until

Rain-freshened rhododendrons surround author
Ron Fisher in Georgia. Enveloped in a poncho, he heads north
on the Appalachian Trail, white-blazed along its
2,100 miles and intermittently marked with the A.T. monogram,
above. Some four million hikers a year travel a portion of
the route, which stretches from Georgia to Maine.

October. His mother and father are a little worried, because of the snow. "We tried to get him to wait another week," his mother says. Jerry senior adds: "We left the motel this morning and drove out here in a nice warm car, and when we got here . . . Whew! It was cold! Jerry was shaking, it was so cold, but he said, 'I gotta get goin'.' "

"If you run across him," Mrs. Gramling says, "check on his welfare and give us a call. I don't suppose *he* will. He's like most hikers; he wants to be alone." We *would* run across Jerry, and his parents again, too, in the months to come, as we explored the Appalachian Trail.

It was 50 years ago, on August 14, 1937, that a crew of young men in the Civilian Conservation Corps, the CCC, stitched together the final segment of the Appalachian Trail, clearing and blazing a two-mile-long section on the north slope of Spaulding Mountain, in Maine. It was the last link in a wilderness footpath that runs from Georgia to Maine.

The trail's origins date back even farther, into the twenties. The father is generally considered to be Benton MacKaye, a conservationist from Shirley Center, Massachusetts. The October 1921 issue of the *Journal of the American Institute of Architects* carried his article, "An Appalachian Trail, a Project in Regional Planning." "It fortunately happens," he wrote, "that we have throughout the most densely populated portion of the United States a fairly continuous belt of underdeveloped lands. These are contained in the several ranges which form the Appalachian chain of mountains. . . . What is suggested, therefore, is a 'long trail' over the full length of the Appalachian skyline, from the highest peak in the north to the highest peak in the south. . . . Each section should be in the immediate charge of a local group of people." These broad outlines of MacKaye's proposal have been realized, even to the use of volunteers to build and maintain the trail. "Here is enormous undeveloped power," MacKaye had written, "the spare time of our population." The "spare time" that volunteers devoted to the Appalachian Trail in 1987 alone amounted to tens of thousands of hours.

Back on Springer, we continue upward through the snow. Much of the forest looks devastated. Freshly broken branches and treetops litter the ground, broken off within the last few days by the heavy, wet snow. The wounds, pale against the dark branches, look raw and painful. White as the snow but obviously man-made, paint blazes on the occasional tree mark the trail in both directions. They're meant to be uniform—each two by six inches, each at eye level, each on a tree that "strikes the eye." Blazes are placed frequently enough that one is usually visible, and two blazes, one above the other, warn hikers of an unusual change of direction. Blue blazes mark side trails. "Painted neatly," says a manual on trail design, construction, and maintenance, "with sharp corners and clean edges, the blaze is easy both to discern from a distance and to distinguish from natural marks." Anywhere between Georgia and Maine, the blazes are as reassuring as old friends, seeming to beckon and say, "This way."

The trail was once defined by the Appalachian Trail Conference, its

FRASER'S FIR *(Abies fraseri)*

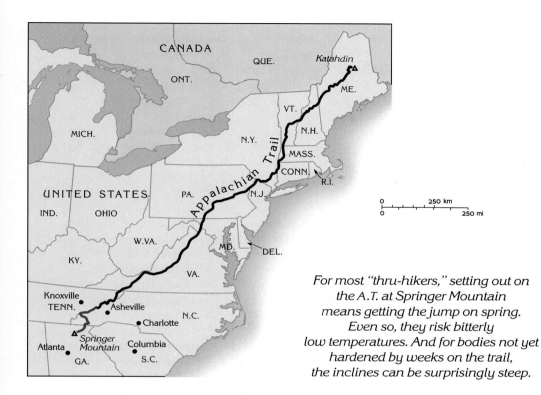

For most "thru-hikers," setting out on the A.T. at Springer Mountain means getting the jump on spring. Even so, they risk bitterly low temperatures. And for bodies not yet hardened by weeks on the trail, the inclines can be surprisingly steep.

parent organization, thus: "The Appalachian Trail (A.T.) is a continuous, marked footpath extending from Katahdin, a granite monolith in the central Maine wilderness, some 2,100 miles south to Springer Mountain, in Georgia. It is a skyliner route along the crest of the ranges generally referred to as 'Appalachian,' hence the name of the Trail."

The Appalachian Trail Conference, or the ATC, was founded in 1925 to promote interest in the trail, to determine the route, and to coordinate its development and maintenance. The conference today has about 22,000 members. Additionally, some 60 affiliated trail clubs have about 60,000 members. Scattered up and down the length of the trail, many of these members are the volunteers who work to maintain the A.T. The ATC has overall responsibility for trail construction, maintenance, management, and protection; it publishes guidebooks and maps of the trail; it conducts education and research projects related to the trail; it serves as liaison among the many public and private organizations and individuals involved with the trail; and five times a year it publishes the *Appalachian Trailway News,* a witty and informative magazine of trail doings.

The ATC has a board of managers, which functions much as any board of directors. In 1979, it issued its thoughts on what the trail ought always be: "The Appalachian Trail in its entirety shall be kept forever open, obvious, and narrowly passable for hiking. The treadway shall pass lightly over the land to provide for the least disturbance to the natural setting. The Trail shall be marked and cleared to offer passage that may be both enjoyable for the reasonably prepared and in harmony with the natural environment."

That phrase "reasonably prepared" worried me the first time I saw it, and it came back to haunt me on a number of occasions later.

Finally reaching the summit of Springer, at 3,782 feet, we find a bronze plaque embedded in a boulder, showing a hiker striding up a mountain. Near him, we stand and look through leafless trees out onto the Blue Ridge. From here, many hikers who expect to walk the entire trail pick up a pebble to carry to Maine.

S am and I established a routine these first few days in Georgia that would carry us through the spring, summer, and fall. We did some lengthy hikes, as well as short day hikes, and we dropped in on some interesting people and places where the trail touches highways.

For instance, we stopped by the post office in Suches, Georgia, where postmistress Andrea Verner was firmly in charge. Hikers who plan to walk the whole distance—"thru-hikers," they're called—must of necessity plan the logistics of their trips carefully. To maintain a steady flow of supplies, at the outset they mail boxes of food to themselves at various post offices near the trail. The first post office easily accessible to hikers after leaving Springer is in Suches, about 20 miles into their trip. By the time they reach Andrea's post office, they have begun to lighten their packs, discarding and mailing home the heavy items that seemed like essentials when they set out. "People come in here to get packages they've sent to themselves," said Andrea, chuckling, "and usually they send home more than they pick up. They'll come in with 80 pounds in their packs and go out with 50. Last year a boy mailed home a Russian army helmet. The thing weighed 22 pounds. Two boys last week came in out of the rain and emptied their packs right there in the lobby. Everything was soaking wet. Customers could barely get through, but it was so cold I didn't have the heart to throw the hikers out. They mailed big packages of wet clothes home to their mothers. Sent them by parcel post, so it was four or five days before they got there. What a mess!

"They're a crazy bunch, these hikers. They make up these outlandish trail names for themselves and then ask about each other. They'll say, 'Have you seen Grasshopper?' Well *really!*"

North of Suches, the A.T. in Georgia keeps mostly to ridges of some 3,500 feet above sea level, with steep ups and downs. Views from rocky outcrops are of gently contoured mountains, the southern extremity of the Blue Ridge. Mount Oglethorpe, farther south, was once the southern terminus of the A.T. But private development, including chicken farms, began to encroach seriously on the trail in the fifties, so in 1958 the ATC abandoned Oglethorpe to the developers and moved the terminus north to Springer, where it has since been. Now, almost the entire length of the A.T. in Georgia, 78 miles, lies within the Chattahoochee National Forest. The trail was built by the U.S. Forest Service in the thirties and for the most part is in its original location. These Georgia mountains are justly famed for their blazing

AMERICAN MOUNTAIN ASH *(Sorbus americana)*

spring displays of rhododendrons, mountain laurel, and flame azaleas.

Over the course of the next few days, I made a number of forays into the woods, both here and farther along the trail in North Carolina. The weather stayed nice: cool enough for hiking, warm enough for resting on trailside boulders. After a long winter, the forest was coming back to life.

On Easter morning, I went for a walk along the trail near Suches, heading north from Woody Gap. Patches of snow were gradually melting into the dark forest floor. The trees were still bare of leaves, and the views through the forest were spacious. Sounds carried clearly. I could hear hikers behind me: "Is all the trail this well maintained?" someone asked his companion. No, I might have answered. I stopped to let them pass. First came a golden retriever with a bright red bandanna around its neck, then a frolicky black pup, then two people. Ten minutes later I could still hear them, far out in front of me.

Signs of spring abounded: hikers in shorts; birds singing in treetops; small white wildflowers in a sunny spot between two hills; a few bugs and gnats; a towhee, singing. From somewhere came the drumming of pileated woodpeckers. I caught an occasional glimpse of them—flashes of red and white darting through the treetops.

Soon I met a large red-faced woman carrying her dog, a tiny hairless thing, and a few minutes later along came a man with two dogs, one wearing bulging orange saddlebags. When Saddlebags saw that her master and I were going to spend a few minutes talking, she knelt and wriggled backward out of her harness, slipping the pack over her head, then rolled luxuriously in the leaves. She weighed 33 pounds, I was told, and her pack weighed 10, mostly dog food. The ATC recommends against taking dogs on the A.T., and a few minutes later I heard one reason why: the angry shouts and hysterical barking of a dogfight. Red Bandanna meets Orange Saddlebags!

On a rocky outcrop atop Big Cedar Mountain, I sat and munched nuts and seeds and raisins—the ubiquitous "gorp"—and watched two hawks swooping and climbing over the valley. They were either fighting or courting; with hawks, it's not always easy to tell. They dived and grappled in midair. Once, as their talons locked, the lower one turned over and flew on its back. They climbed higher and higher, backed by clouds and blue sky, until I could barely hear their faint pips. When they were mere specks, they suddenly turned themselves into stones and dropped straight down. Down and down. My binoculars jerked as I tried to keep them in view. At treetop level they turned into birds again, and soared.

The Georgia roads and highways that cross the trail do so in the "gaps"—notches that are vitally important as openings in the Appalachian wall. To drive through them today is to be struck again by the solid, timeless beauty of these ancient mountains. On still mornings, fingers of mist rise from valleys and drift among the trees. Squatting at roadsides are tough little country stores doubling as gas stations. One has a sign out front offering "Crickets and Worms."

At the next gap up the trail—Neels Gap—spring was much on the mind of Dorothy Hansen, who with her husband, Jeff, runs the Walasi-Yi Center, a handsome old stone building whose name meant "the place of frogs" to the Cherokees. The inn offers car shuttles, showers, meals, and overnight facilities to hikers, as well as camping and backpacking supplies. "It's been an unusual spring," Dorothy told me. "It was in the sixties back in March, and now this: two feet of snow. We've had a couple of cases of borderline hypothermia, hikers caught out in it. The first night we had 30 snowbound backpackers here. I was up till three in the morning doing I don't know how many loads of laundry. There's been a large number of hikers, too. Most years we have maybe 100 through here by this time. This year we've had 250."

Spring is the time of wildflowers in the Appalachians. One warm, sunny morning Donald W. Pfitzer, of the U.S. Fish and Wildlife Service, took a number of us for a stroll through the woods a few miles from the trail, in search of early flowers. Among those we found that day was trailing arbutus, a small plant with pale pink flowers. It is also known as mayflower, perhaps for the month of the year, though it blooms here much earlier than that. Maybe an old legend has it right: When the Pilgrims first came ashore in New England, the first flower they saw was the trailing arbutus, so in gratitude they called it the mayflower after the ship that had brought them safely to America. We unexpectedly came across a patch of white jonquils blooming where they had been planted in a yard now long vanished deep in the forest. For 50 years or so they had been faithfully blooming here, long after whoever planted them had disappeared and the forest had reclaimed the house and farm.

Small houses of another sort have been built, generally by volunteers, along the A.T. Each of these shelters is about a day's walk from the last. Typically, they are three-sided log, board, or stone structures with a sleeping platform and sometimes bunks, and with a fireplace out front. They offer shelter from rain and wind, and each usually has a spring or other water source nearby, walls often thick with graffiti, and an extended family of resident mice. Most shelters will hold at least six hikers but seldom more than twelve.

The Plumorchard Gap Shelter is about 4½ miles from the highway in Dicks Creek Gap, and I walked in to it on the first day of May.

A revolution in backpacking equipment during the last few years enabled me to carry everything I needed for a night in the woods—food, water, cooking equipment, sleeping bag and pad, rain gear, spare clothing, basic medical supplies, even a tent in case the shelter was full—in a light, sturdy pack. The total weight probably did not exceed 30 pounds. And, because man does not live by gorp alone, I even carried a small canteen of wine, which, laid to rest in the spring, would cool delightfully by suppertime.

The snow was finally gone, and the treetops were merry with the songs of warblers migrating through. The forest, still bare of leaves, resounded with their chirps and whistles. Here and there the dogwoods were blooming, each little tree ablaze with dazzling white blossoms. The flowers were so white and the twigs and branches so black and invisible that the blossoms looked disembodied, as if they were floating in air.

At the shelter, which nestles near a spring on a hillside, another dogwood was in bloom, just where a porch might have been. Scarlet tanagers, bumblebees, and chickadees worked the local trees and bushes into the late afternoon, and a brief sprinkle filled the air with moisture. Inside the shelter, on a wall, someone had written, "If home is where the heart is, I never left." At dusk, three white-tailed deer came to the spring for a drink. You could just hear them rustling the underbrush as they tiptoed through the forest. After their drink, they moseyed past the shelter, stopping now and then to look me over, their tails flicking, their big ears aimed like dish antennas. The next morning I awoke to sunshine and the sounds of birds singing. Later I heard a crash in the woods and looked up to see a hawk taking off, empty-taloned. Somewhere nearby there was a chipmunk, I'll wager, thanking its lucky stars.

The Appalachian Trail touches or passes through 14 states, as well as 6 areas managed by the National Park Service and 8 national forests. The National Trails System Act that was passed in 1968 first gave the trail official protection and also authorized the acquisition of rights-of-way, by easement, by purchase, by exchange, or—a final possibility—by condemnation. Ten years later, in 1978, an amendment to the act emphasized the need to proceed more quickly with protection of the A.T. The amendment included authorization for the acquisition of a corridor averaging a thousand feet in width. At that time, Congress approved the appropriation of 90 million dollars for acquiring the land or the rights-of-way. Today, nearly 80 percent of the needed acreage has been acquired. It is protected under the broad and benign umbrella of the National Park Service in cooperation with the U.S. Forest Service and other federal, state, and local jurisdictions.

David M. Sherman is one of the country's most determined and thoughtful supporters of the Appalachian Trail. Born and reared in Georgia, Dave has worked for the Department of the Interior since the mid-seventies, where he fought hard for measures that expanded the protection of the A.T. He not only has hiked the entire trail but also has worked toward federal acquisition of adjacent tracts considered essential to the trail's protection. "The Appalachians were the first major barrier to westward expansion," Dave had reminded me, back in Washington. "They've long since been conquered, and now in some places the 'vast wilderness' referred to in accounts of early travelers will survive only as the thousand-foot-wide corridor for the Appalachian Trail. What is being preserved today is probably in many places all that will survive of the forest that helped make the Appalachians formidable. We simply must protect the best of what is left, so future generations will be able to get some flavor of the eastern mountain wilderness that seemed such an obstacle to the early explorers."

Crossing the state line into North Carolina, a hiker comes into the Nantahala Mountains. They have a grander look, a rougher and meaner aspect than the Georgia mountains. Their (Continued on page 32)

FOLLOWING PAGES: Encasing twig and branch in glistening ice, rime highlights ridges of North Carolina's Nantahala National Forest. Here, where the trail ascends to more than 5,000 feet, spring sunshine can quickly give way to snow and sleet.

SYD NISBET

RED FLOWERING DOGWOOD *(Cornus florida f. rubra)*

CHRIS JOHNS (ALL)

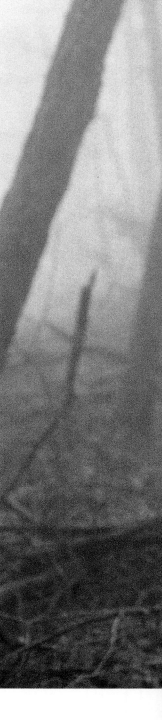

His face revealing the agony of a 75-pound pack and new boots,
Scott Grierson plods through foggy April drizzle toward the summit
of Springer Mountain. His goal: Maine by September. One of
several hundred aspiring thru-hikers annually, Scott bids farewell
to friends (opposite, upper) who drove him to the trailhead.
At the summit, he commits his quest to writing as he signs the register.

Vermilion sun dips
toward a horizon of the
rolling Blue Ridge.
Blood Mountain,
highest point
of the Appalachian Trail
in Georgia, rewards
visitors with
this panoramic
view. According to Indian
legend, the mountain
got its name after
a fierce battle
there between
Cherokees and Creeks.

Holding a piece of yellowroot, a common streamside plant
early settlers used to treat sore throats, Don Pfitzer
leads a botany walk at Unicoi State Park, Georgia. In the
southern Appalachians, abundant rainfall and variations in
soil, sunlight, and elevation nurture the greatest
variety of flowering plants in North America. A garden
of diversity thrives on a mountainside in North Carolina (below).
Amid ferns and wild geranium foliage, large-flowered
trilliums bloom near the long-stemmed buds
of Clinton's lily; mayapples raise their miniature umbrellas.

© DAVID MUENCH 1988 (ABOVE); CHRIS JOHNS (RIGHT)

*Appalachian Trail passes through
a breezeway at Walasi-Yi Center. Built by
the Civilian Conservation Corps,
it straddles the route at
Neels Gap, Georgia. Below, death
nurtures life: A conifer seedling
springs from a decaying log.*

*FOLLOWING PAGES: Lookout tower atop
Mount Cammerer, just half a
mile from the trail, affords panoramic
vistas of Great Smoky
Mountains National Park.*

(Continued from page 19) peaks are higher, the highway curves that loop around them are longer, and the valleys seem deeper. There's a place here where the trail goes steadily uphill for most of eight grueling miles.

Virtually all of the A.T. from the Georgia line to the Great Smoky Mountains National Park lies within the Nantahala National Forest, made up of stands of mature hardwoods with rhododendrons, flame azaleas, mountain laurel, mountain ash, and beds of fern and galax. In spring, wildflowers bloom in ever changing profusion, and streams and springs gurgle with abundant water. Once this was Indian country, home to the beleaguered Cherokees, who were driven from their homelands in 1838. Old Highway 64 in Wallace Gap was once an Indian trading route and later a colonial road. I crossed it when I hiked south from Winding Stair Gap to Rock Gap Shelter.

At the shelter, the inevitable mice darted in and out of cracks between the stones of the fireplace. A hiker once facetiously suggested that cats be installed at the shelters, not only to control the mice but also to serve as companions for lonely backpackers and to clean up leftovers.

On one wall was a note from the Nantahala Hiking Club urging hikers to boil the water. "We have been advised that purification tablets are not effective against certain organisms." Hmmm. It's *Giardia lamblia* they're talking about, a protozoan that causes an intestinal disorder called giardiasis in humans. Even though streams or springs may *look* clean, animals can contaminate even the remotest of them.

The trail proper was about 150 feet away from the shelter, down a side trail. In the night, on the verge of sleep, I heard voices. Two men were on the trail, making their way carefully through the darkness, reassuring each other. "Here's a blaze," one said. "We're still okay." They spotted the shelter in the darkness, and we shouted back and forth a bit. They weren't stopping, they said. Their destination was a campground another mile down the trail. As they moved on, I could hear them talking. "It's so dark I couldn't tell if that was the shelter or not," one said. "I could see the white of the roof, but at first I thought it was just a big dogwood in bloom." How about that, I thought, as I dropped off. I'm sleeping in a house that looks like flowers.

As the A.T. approaches the Nantahala River, it drops from 5,000-foot summits and 4,000-foot gaps to about 1,700 feet at the Nantahala Outdoor Center, which runs rafting and kayaking trips on rivers in the area.

From high on the A.T., the Nantahala Gorge looks bottomless. The forest is dry and sunny on top but darker and more moist lower down. I had barely started descending when I saw a snake beside the trail. About four feet long, it was black with a white chin. A rat snake. Its quivering tail vibrated against some dry leaves, making a faint rustling noise. As its tongue flicked in my direction, I leaned over and addressed it: "You can probably fool some of the people," I said, "but you can't fool me: You're no rattlesnake."

Down, down, down. As I descend toward the river, the air gets cooler and the vegetation becomes greener. I begin to hear water trickling here and there, and I walk through clusters of rhododendrons and mountain laurel. Down, down, down. The forest floor itself is now damp as the canopy overhead thickens. I round a bend and hear rapids in the river still far below. There's moss on the stones and boulders, and the birds, when they sing, sound high up and far away. Split-log bridges a couple of feet wide cross the wet corners of the switchbacks, and there's usually a trickle of water there. The light has failed, and it's dark in the forest. Finally, I can look down through trees and see the tops of trucks going by on the highway and flowering trees on the shoulders.

At the south end of the Great Smokies, the trail stubs its toe on a massive concrete structure—Fontana Dam. A project of the Tennessee Valley Authority, or TVA, the dam was built during World War II as a source of hydroelectric power. A 29-mile-long lake has piled up behind it. The trail follows the top of the dam, with the lake on one side, the Little Tennessee River 480 feet below on the other.

Swallows were thick and noisy along the face of the dam, plucking bugs from the cool concrete the day I crossed. About midway I came to a sign: "No Visitors Beyond This Point." Workmen with drills were inserting metal reinforcing rods into the concrete to strengthen it. "We let hikers cross," one told me, "but no cars." So I crossed the rest of the way rather quickly.

At the park headquarters, near Gatlinburg—where I stocked up on T-shirts and fudge—I talked with Bob Wightman, who at the time was the north district backcountry ranger. The Great Smoky Mountains National Park is one of the few sections of the A.T. where hikers need worry about permits and reservations. They're a nuisance for everyone, but they became a necessary evil a few years ago. "Back in the mid-seventies," Bob said, "backpacking became a real fad. Not only were there more people out there on the trails, but also there were more people who didn't know what they were doing. Shelters were frequently overcrowded. So we instituted a system of permits and reservations, and space at the shelters is rationed. Only a thru-hiker—which we define as someone who starts at least 50 miles outside the park, hikes through, and goes at least 50 miles on the other side—can pass through without giving us an itinerary. We reserve a few bunks in each of the shelters along the A.T. for thru-hikers from mid-April to mid-June. The rest of the time we treat them like everyone else."

The Appalachian Trail stays above 5,000 feet for nearly half the distance through the park. The highest point on the entire A.T. is Clingmans Dome, the crest of the Smokies, at 6,643 feet.

Sam and I set out from the trailhead in Newfound Gap. For much of our hike, we would follow the North Carolina–Tennessee border. As we began our trek in the Smokies, thunder boomed like artillery barrages. The trail was already damp from showers. Sprinkles came and went, and rain threatened all afternoon, resurrecting a perennial backpacking question: At what point do you stop and take the trouble to dig out your poncho and pack cover? And why do the sprinkles always stop as soon as you do?

It took 15 or 20 minutes for the sounds of traffic to fade behind us, and then the woods were still, with only the sounds of water dripping from the trees. When the sun came out, the forest filled with fog. We reached Icewater Spring Shelter in time to escape the heavy downpour late in the afternoon.

FRASER'S MAGNOLIA (Magnolia fraseri)

Ten people shared the shelter that night, and I spent some time visiting with a North Carolina man. Because of his heavy accent, I could barely understand him, and—this was a shock—*he* could barely understand *me*.

Much of the route the next day ran along the sharp crest of The Sawteeth, a ridge sometimes little more than ten yards wide. This section of the trail was built back in the thirties by the CCC, and the stonework remains strong and beautiful. Juncos nested in the grass below, and rhododendrons bloomed overhead. At four o'clock, the pattern held: Safely in Pecks Corner Shelter, we had another rainstorm.

The next morning, we walked a soppy trail through a wet forest. Snails left glittering trails on the path, and jets overhead traced contrails in the sky. Because the A.T. starts near Atlanta—a huge transportation hub—and runs north along the edge of the East Coast megalopolis, there is seldom a time when you can't either see or hear an airplane.

Late in the morning, while I was sitting alongside the trail having a snack, a doe came along. She peered at me, flicked her tail, then stepped daintily off into the bushes. I thought at first she might have wanted some gorp, but probably she just wanted me to move so she could use the trail.

We arrived at Tricorner Knob Shelter in midafternoon, had a half-bath under a pipe in the spring, and were making coffee when the day's storm rolled in, an especially fierce one. Lightning exploded like flashbulbs, thunder hammered at the metal roof, and the rain came down in buckets.

We had been warned of an aggressive mouse at this shelter. A hiker had hung his food bag from an overhead beam here, after having carefully threaded the line through an upside-down tin can, but the mouse managed to get into the bag anyway. The hiker could hear it in there during the night, eating crackers. Finally he got up, got some of the crackers, made a pile of them on the floor, and went back to bed. But the mouse—a perverse creature—ignored the feast laid for it and went straight back into the food bag.

No mouse showed for us, but a bear came along. Shelters in the Smokies have as their fourth wall a barrier of heavy wire, designed specifically to keep out bears. It's a little like being in a reverse zoo, with the animals on the outside looking in. Sure enough, just at dusk, a bear came and sauntered back and forth with a pigeon-toed gait and glittering black eyes. It lay down in front of the door and put its nose beneath the wire. *Sniff sniff.* It flinched at the sound of a zipper, then a flashbulb frightened it away.

Alongside the trail in the morning, there was evidence of wild hogs. Badly disturbed areas looked as if someone had been working with a garden tiller. The wild hogs of the Smokies, descendants of boars imported for hunting early in the century, today number perhaps 1,500 and are nearly impossible to eradicate.

The shelter that night—Cosby Knob—was crowded. One young man there had stayed in this very shelter on his very first camping trip some years before. It was crowded then, too. He had slept on the floor near the fireplace and, during the chilly night, had fed sticks into the fire, including—he discovered in the morning—everybody's walking stick. Some of the sticks were sentimental favorites. "One guy wanted to kill me," he remembered.

Talk among the hikers was of routes, terrain, miles, weather, and—of endless interest—boots and food. One kid from New York, who had been on the trail for several weeks, hoped that in Waterville, a six-house hamlet near Davenport Gap, he could buy a bagel. We weren't encouraging.

The next morning I found an old horseshoe on the trail, and a few minutes later met a party of riders. This section in the Smokies is one of the few places where horses are allowed on the Appalachian Trail. One of the horses was slightly spooked as it passed me, and its rider reassured it: "Whoa," he said. "That ain't no booger"—meaning *me*.

For the last afternoon of our hike in the Smokies, we walked downhill, descending some 3,500 feet over a distance of 9 miles. As we dropped down through the different ecological zones, the rhododendrons grew bigger and their blossoms more mature. About midday we reached the elevation where galax flourishes. It's a low-growing evergreen plant whose leaves turn a lovely bronze color in the fall.

We made our final descent along Big Creek, following a short trail through a dark and green stretch of forest where mosses and ferns thrive. Sam compared it to being in the bottom of a terrarium.

Because of the nature of Appalachian geography, nearly every hike along the A.T. ends at a highway. And this one was no different. Practically every hike, too, ends with a twinge of melancholy, mixed with gladness: The hard, sweaty work is finished, but so is the solitude; you can get a decent meal, but you can't share it with a chipmunk; you can sleep in a soft bed, but you can't see the stars.

I thought of one of those old hymns, another that might have been addressed to hikers: "Tho' the hills be steep and the valleys deep, With no flow'rs my way adorning; Tho' the night be lone and my rest a stone, Joy awaits me in the morning." ☐

WILD STRAWBERRY *(Fragaria virginiana)*

FOLLOWING PAGES: Gauzy mist cloaks hillside and hollow in the Great Smoky Mountains. Dense stands of hemlock and spruce and beech and maple flourish in the region's moderate temperatures and long growing season.

35

FRED J. ALSOP III

*Out on a limb, a black bear seems
to defy gravity as it seeks a viewpoint in the
Smokies. Trail shelters here have a heavy
wire wall to keep bears and
hikers apart. Above, a male northern
oriole feeds its young. Lungless
red salamanders (below) breathe through
their skin and mouth lining.*

ANIMALS ANIMALS/ZIG LESZCZYNSKI (ABOVE); © SONJA BULLATY & ANGELO LOMEO (RIGHT)

*Virgin forest of red spruce
surrounds author Fisher as he hikes
in the Smokies. Trailside
enchantments range from such giant
patriarch trees to the delicate
blossoms of lady's slipper (below).*

*FOLLOWING PAGES: Golden ragwort
carpets Engine Gap, a meadow in
the Roan highlands.*

MIKE WARREN

SYD NISBET

41

Silent Forests, Gentle Voices

This classified ad appeared in the *Appalachian Trailway News* not long ago: "For Sale—Hiking boots, size 9½, used only 32 miles. . . ." There's a story there, a story of a hike: of plans, of high expectations and eager anticipation, of the first buoyant steps, of puzzling hot spots on toes and heels, finally of actual blisters, of misery, of *blood,* of solemn vows never to go hiking again. "For Sale—Gortex/leather hiking boots, Austrian made. Kastinger Pacifics, size 10½, worn once. . . ."

The *Trailway News* is a window into the minds of backpackers, who, as Andrea the postmistress said, are a crazy bunch. They use its pages to learn about relocations of the A.T. or about new side trails, to swap everything from equipment to recipes, to read features on trail clubs and trail personalities and on the latest in equipment and food. In "Public Notices," they locate hiking partners or lost sunglasses.

A column called "Along the Trail" reports on the doings of individuals, clubs, and government agencies. In it I read about the golden anniversary of the Chattahoochee National Forest: "Special events on July 7 and 8 included music, displays, and refreshments atop Brasstown Bald, Georgia's highest mountain. . . ." And, on another subject: "The effects of gypsy moth infestation have become visible in the mid-Atlantic area, particularly in Pennsylvania, Maryland, and northern Virginia. Denuded oak trees show up as patches of brown on otherwise green mountainsides."

The *Trailway News* has been published since 1939 and now reaches more than 22,000 readers. Spend much time in its pages, and you discover that, as much as the A.T. is about woods and wildlife, it is also about people. In the stretch of trail from the Smokies on north through the Blue Ridge, I would be moving through an old and settled region and would come across folksy old men, politicians, scientists, and warm and welcoming

Dappled coat of a whitetail fawn helps hide it
from predators. Close encounters with a diversity of wild
creatures add to the trail's magic. Carved into a tree,
the A.T. emblem (above) indicates the path.

townspeople—all having some connection with the Appalachian Trail.

North of the Great Smokies, Hot Springs, North Carolina, straddles the A.T., which makes its way through the town on U.S. Routes 25 and 70. The some 700 townspeople had been planning a homecoming for former residents and had turned the event into a three-day fete that would include a commemoration of the A.T.'s 50th anniversary. A beauty pageant, a sock hop, a reunion at the high school, a community church service, music, crafts, and entertainment would all be part of the festivities. The A.T. event would be held on Sunday afternoon on the lawn of the Jesuit Residence. For years, the Jesuits have maintained a clean, warm, and dry hostel for hikers next door to their residence—and barely ten yards from the A.T.

I arrived in time for the open-air church service on Main Street and its Bible lesson from the book of *Ruth:* "Whither thou goest . . . ," which seemed appropriate. After church I had a Trail Burger at the Trail Cafe, then listened for a while to gospel singers next door: "There is a river we must cross," they sang, and, "I shall not be able, Lord, to walk the narrow way."

Later I found a shady spot on the lawn of the Jesuit Residence and made myself comfortable. A small, freckled Boy Scout led us in the Pledge of Allegiance to the flag. A true son of the South, he managed to make of "indivisible" an eight-syllable word: "ee-unh-duh-vee-uh-suh-bull-uh."

Among the speakers was Raymond Hunt, chairman of the ATC board of managers. He recalled three important accomplishments from the trail's past. "First, there have been 50 years of maintenance," he said. "Little trees grow into big trees, big trees that always seem to fall down across the trail. I expect that the A.T. has been entirely rebuilt 20 or 30 times since its completion in 1937. Second, relocations. The trail has been moved countless times, and practically every relocation makes it slightly longer. For the moment, it is 2,109.5 miles. And three, after years of trying, we're close to achieving a protected corridor for the trail." He went on to list goals for the next 50 years: more recognition and awareness from the nonhiking public; maintaining a strong working relationship with the ATC's official partners, especially the Forest Service and the Park Service; and the control of threats to the trail, such as development, roads, logging, open areas growing over.

There were half a dozen speakers, and I was interested to note the different ways they pronounced "Appalachian." There's a line across the country—somewhere in Virginia, I think—where the pronunciation changes. North of the line it's Apple-ATE-chun; in the south it's Apple-AT-chun.

James McClure Clarke, the area's representative in the U.S. Congress, was firmly in the Apple-AT-chun camp. He made an interesting point, I thought. "The maintaining of the Appalachian Trail," he said, "may be the largest volunteer effort in support of a recreation facility anywhere on earth."

A number of thru-hikers, on their way north, were sprinkled throughout the audience. Appropriately, there on the Jesuit lawn, several looked like biblical prophets: ragged, bearded, carrying long staffs.

For another 180 miles, the trail makes its way toward Virginia, much of it

SOURWOOD *(Oxydendrum arboreum)*

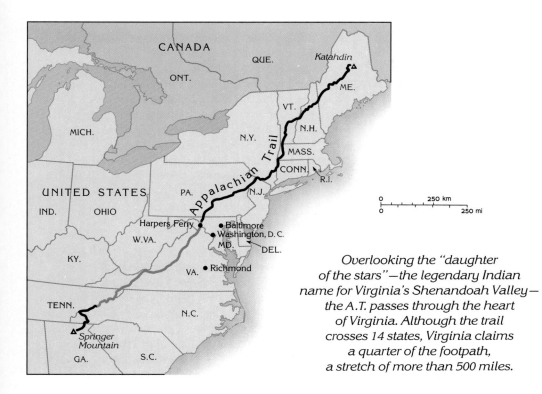

Overlooking the "daughter of the stars"—the legendary Indian name for Virginia's Shenandoah Valley— the A.T. passes through the heart of Virginia. Although the trail crosses 14 states, Virginia claims a quarter of the footpath, a stretch of more than 500 miles.

following the Tennessee–North Carolina border. Near Coldspring Mountain, history-buff hikers find a poignant trailside monument: a single grave with tombstones at each end commemorating William and David Shelton, nephew and uncle. They left their homes in North Carolina to enlist in the Union forces early in the Civil War. Returning home for a reunion with their families, they and a young boy, a lookout, were ambushed and killed by Confederates. All three were buried here in a single grave. The markers were placed in 1915 by two local pastors, but since money for them had come from federal funds, only the soldiers were honored.

The character of these southern mountains was largely formed at the end of the most recent ice age, some 12,000 years ago, when a spruce-fir forest covered much of the area. As the climate warmed, broad-leaved hardwoods moved into the mountains from the south, and the red spruce and Fraser's fir moved up-slope to the mountaintops, where they remain today.

Individual mountain ranges became something like islands, many retaining their unique plants and animals. Salamanders, for instance, tend to differ from range to range, and ravens, juncos, and certain warblers, essentially northern birds, are at home on these cool southern peaks. Geographer Arnold Guyot tramped through them just before the Civil War, making the first recorded climbs of many and refining a technique using a barometer to determine their elevations.

For me, one of the most memorable sections of the entire A.T. is in

47

Tennessee—the 2.7 miles of trail running through the rugged gorge of Laurel Fork. Both rhododendrons and mountain laurel were in bloom, making cool splashes of white in the dark forest. Laurel Falls tumbles 40 feet over a rocky cliff. Heavily wooded walls rise more than 1,200 feet on either side.

Later on the trail, a woodchuck waddled along before me, and then a mother grouse exploded with a squawk from alongside the trail. She flapped off and settled 50 feet away. I took a few more steps, and up popped four chicks, uttering panicky *eeks*. Flying, they looked perfectly round, like feathered tennis balls. They scattered, each settling into the tall grass some distance from the others, but I could hear the whole family chirping signals as they reassembled.

One thing I've noticed on long hikes: Since walking is pretty automatic, there's nothing to do for hours on end but *think,* and that afternoon I got to thinking about backpacks. About how, if they're too heavy, they can take over, emptying your head of everything but their presence and making the trip an endurance test. Supported by hips and shoulders, they lurch this way and that. Even the lightest, after a while, clings like a live creature and seems to whisper in your ear, "This isn't fun; it's work. Give it up." A hiker's fantasy revenge: "For Sale—Backpack, like new. . . ."

Two miles from Damascus, Virginia, you begin to hear an occasional truck on Virginia Route 716, and later, as you work your way downward toward the town, you may hear the sudden sound of a horn honking or of a child playing. You round a corner and suddenly roofs are visible below, through the trees. You can see into someone's backyard—clothes on the line, a doghouse, an upset water dish. Then you're on a street and a dog comes yapping at your heels. You'd think the dogs of Damascus, of all places, would be accustomed to hikers passing through their town. The temperature, you note, seems 20 degrees higher here than it was up on the ridge half an hour ago. You turn right on Laurel Avenue and cross Beaverdam Creek. You feel a little self-conscious, walking down a sidewalk in town wearing a backpack. Everyone else is driving. The white blazes are on utility poles.

Damascus is some 450 miles north of Springer Mountain and about a fifth of the way to Maine. It, like the town of Hot Springs, back in North Carolina, was planning a celebration for the A.T.'s 50th anniversary.

Damascus has long had the reputation among hikers as the friendliest town on the A.T. Its Corner Cafe can rustle up the sort of cheeseburger and milk shake that backpackers dream about; its Methodist Church runs a hostel that welcomes hikers; and for 28 years it had a postmaster famous the whole length of the trail. Until he retired in 1985, Paschal Grindstaff did all he could—and more—to ease the passage of hikers through his town. "Nothing is more rewarding," he once wrote, "than to deliver a letter from a loved one to a tired hiker who has been weeks on the Trail." Hikers could depend on him to watch over their waiting food parcels, to respond to queries from anxious parents, to offer solace and advice to weary walkers.

I dropped by the City Shoe Shop to see another legend, cobbler Shorty

FLAME AZALEA *(Rhododendron calendulaceum)*

Stout, who reminded me of the cobbler in *Pinocchio.* A gray-and-white house cat lay sprawled on the counter, idly playing with the laces of a boot. A guest book, also on the counter, was filled with testimonials from satisfied customers. A traditionalist, Shorty doesn't think much of boots made of "that newfangled synthetic stuff." During the height of the hiking season, he often repairs four or five pairs of boots a day. He prides himself on getting hikers reshod and back on the trail. He also repairs their packs when they break. I asked him what gets hikers in trouble, boot-wise. "Well," he said, "a lot of 'em, when their soles start comin' off, try to glue 'em on themselves. They just don't hold. I had one fella a while back, I was just closin' on Saturday night, he came in with a sole ripped clean off. He had wored it."

"Had what?"

"Had wropped it with a piece of wore. I put my apron back on, sat down, and had 'im on the trail next mornin'."

Shorty's shop overlooked the parade a few days later during the town's Appalachian Trail celebration. It was a short but eclectic parade, led by a contingent of U.S. Navy Seabees (who had been working nearby on another trail, the Virginia Creeper). They were followed by a high school band, Miss Appalachian Trail, Cub Scouts and Girl Scouts with lots of flags, Smokey Bear and Woodsy Owl in the back of a Forest Service truck, backpackers, a high school choir, horses, and fire trucks. Postmaster Grindstaff, recently retired, was there, looking fit and happy.

I had some barbecued chicken at the firehouse, then made my way to the hostel, where a speakers' platform had been set up on the lawn. I noted again that day, with relief, that A.T. speakers tend to keep their remarks brief. Dave Startzell, executive director of the ATC, reminded us to "rejoice in the existence of the trail." Ray Hunt spoke again, and Rick Boucher, U.S. representative from Virginia's Ninth District, said, "We are fortunate to have this natural treasure in our own backyard." Dave Thomas, founding president of the Mount Rogers Appalachian Trail Club, accepted a donation of a hundred dollars from Damascus schoolchildren. "When children of an elementary school pitch in their nickels and dimes, it gives me great confidence in the future of the Appalachian Trail," he said.

North of Damascus, on rocky crags that reminded me of Scotland, I walked among mountaintops where the last rhododendrons of spring were making their final superlative effort. The A.T. passes through aptly named Rhododendron Gap in the Mount Rogers National Recreation Area (NRA), where large open areas, rocky ridges, and forests surround Virginia's highest peak, 5,729-foot Mount Rogers. The area is patterned by a confusing array of trails—a horse trail, state park trails, multiple-use trails, old trails, new trails, alternate trails, restricted trails. Everyone I met was either lost or had recently been lost or, like me, was about to become lost. But, I found, it's a wondrous place for being lost.

I did a day hike from Grayson Highlands State Park, a small enclave of cloud-swept peaks and more trails that nestles up against the southern boundary of the Mount Rogers NRA. A gravel path led me gently upward across a bald—one of a number of large grassy areas in the otherwise unbroken forest of the southern Appalachians. The Forest Service keeps this particular bald clear, largely through burning and grazing, and some of the creatures whose nibbling helps—free-roaming but semi-tame ponies—stood and watched while I walked among them. They eyed me with mild curiosity, their tails twitching, as I passed.

The Wilburn Ridge Pony Association looks after the ponies. To keep the herd's population stable, they round up some of the animals each autumn and auction them off. The profits go toward herd management and the support of a local rescue squad.

At Rhododendron Gap—a low-slung saddle between Mount Rogers and Pine Mountain—the rhododendrons were in fierce bloom, great clusters of them, hillsides and ridges pink with them. Clouds of mist came and went, sweeping across the mountaintop, creating a now-you-see-'em, now-you-don't show. Individual blossoms, wet from the mist, sparkled. Overhead, branches met to form tunnels of flowers, and blossoms that had fallen turned the trail pink underfoot.

Beyond the gap, the mist and fog gradually cleared. First there was a soft shadow, then a slow sense of something lifting, and suddenly—sunlight! Mount Rogers itself still had its summit buried in the underbelly of a big gray cloud, but distant mountains appeared on the horizon. I walked through a stand of fir trees, their needles soft and silent underfoot, then into a meadow, where cattle—more soldiers in the battle to keep the mountain open—stood and chewed placidly. Each had a bright blue tag in its left ear that looked like a flower. They might have been on their way to the prom. Each gave me that smug bovine look that seems to say: "I'm a cow and glad of it."

Open areas, such as this meadow, are controversial among trail people. Many of them rightly brag of the A.T.'s diverse terrain: forests, meadows, valleys, peaks. The controversy arises because many of the meadows and balds, if left alone, would soon become overgrown with brush, then with trees. Eventually, the argument goes, the entire Appalachian Trail would be through a boring "green tunnel" of mature forest. So should these historically open areas continue to be kept open? And if so, how and by whom? Or should nature be allowed to run its course?

Dave Sherman says: "Diversity is one of the greatest values of the trail. It allows you a constant sense of discovery, of finding something new and unexpected at every turn of the trail, whether it be a meadow or a pasture or just a picturesque barn. Anything that decreases that diversity, such as allowing a bald with a 360-degree view to grow over, diminishes the value of the A.T."

The pages of the *Trailway News* erupted over the issue, as hikers aired their opinions. Ed Garvey, a 74-year-old thru-hiker and respected trail activist who has written extensively about the trail, is firmly on the side of management. He has recommended that the ATC purchase mowing equipment and hire college students to work their way north each summer, mowing as they go along.

Ken Graber, of New Jersey, disagreed: "Mr. Garvey, notice the first four letters in the word 'wilderness.' Nature has a way of recycling itself and is always changing. A meadow is just one phase of this recycling. . . . As some old meadows slowly become new forests, other areas, by the forces of nature (landslide, fire, etc.) become new meadows."

But Allen Poole, of North Carolina, responded: "Surely Mr. Graber would not suggest that we let the gypsy moth, a mechanism of nature, have its way. I for one, do not think we can take a 'hands off' approach. . . . I think the best we can do is work to preserve the scenic beauty and diversity of the A.T., basing management decisions not always on what nature would do, but on what makes the best Trail."

The Forest and Park Services have many years of experience managing balds, by grazing, mowing, cutting, burning, and in some cases by the application of herbicides. Their research and experimentation have yielded a sizable body of know-how, so management is certainly feasible.

A private organization seeking to protect the open areas in the Roan highlands—in eastern Tennessee and western North Carolina—is the Appalachian Highlands Conservancy. Stanley A. Murray, executive director of the group and former chairman of the ATC's board of managers, believes in preserving balds for their diversity of species as well as their beauty.

After finding my way down from Rhododendron Gap, I stopped by the headquarters of the Mount Rogers NRA. The trail runs alongside the building and through the parking lot, and hikers often stop in for maps or information or just to say hello. "What's the first question they ask you?" I put to Eric Smith, the soft-spoken young ranger on duty that day. He thought for a second. "Have you got change for a dollar?"

"What?"

"Most of them want to use the Pepsi machine, so they ask for change."

Back on the trail, as the cool of spring began to turn into the slow, hot days of summer, I continued north. The A.T. here runs mostly through the Jefferson National Forest, where it makes use of farm roads, old logging roads, and even railroad beds left over from the days of heavy lumbering.

The O'Lystery Community Shelter, a picnic pavilion adjacent to Virginia Route 42, is famous among backpackers. The trail runs right past it, and hikers, if they're lucky, sometimes happen along while a picnic is in progress. In the register were a couple of recent entries. "Utterly gorged from a family reunion," one wrote. "Couldn't have picked a better time to go through," wrote another. "Full as a tick. . . ."

I spent a memorable day near here with Andy Layne, a 76-year-old retired electrician who came to typify for me the best of the A.T. volunteers. A member of the Roanoke Appalachian Trail Club, Andy was one of several volunteers working on a trail relocation near Sinking Creek. While the others revegetated an eroded hillside and built a small bridge, Andy and I would construct a stile across a farmer's fence. When the trail relocation became official later in the summer, everything would be ready.

In a pasture full of cows, high on a hilltop, I found Andy with the tools and materials already assembled: some two-by-sixes, some nails, a brace and bit, a saw, a hammer. Jolly and kind, Andy was a perfect partner for a day of working outside in the sunshine. He was fit, strong, and agile, in spite of some recent heart problems. "Had to give up (Continued on page 66)

MOUNTAIN LAUREL (Kalmia latifolia)

MIKE WARREN

*Wild bouquet of Catawba rhododendrons
brightens a heath bald at the summit of Roan Mountain.
Horses grazing on nearby Big Yellow Mountain
(opposite) help preserve the openness of this grassy bald.*

*FOLLOWING PAGES: North America's largest natural
garden of rhododendrons flourishes in the Roan highlands
on the North Carolina–Tennessee line.*

MIKE WARREN

EDWARD SCHELL

Showy flowering dogwood proclaims a succession of springs as the season, like a thru-hiker, moves steadily northward. This truly native American hardwood, found nearly the entire length of the A.T., briefly displays modified leaves that look like petals.

*Double centerline of U.S. 25 and 70
marks the A.T.'s course into
Hot Springs, North Carolina. Favored rest
stop, the Trail Cafe has served up a
hearty breakfast for thru-hikers
Rita Baumgartner and Laura Schilf.
Before setting out again, Rita
applies sun block and Laura adjusts
her pack. Committed to an estimated
five million steps from Georgia
to Maine, the two women find the trail
a "whole different way of life."
"A lot freer," says Rita.*

CHRIS JOHNS (BOTH)

FOLLOWING PAGES: Music for sore limbs, cascading waters of Laurel Falls soothe Michele Miller. The A.T. provides entry to this steep, pristine gorge in Tennessee's Cherokee National Forest.

Younger hikers look out from the porch of The Place,
an A.T. hostel sponsored by the United Methodist Church in Damascus,
Virginia, as Gene Espy recalls his through-trek in 1951: "I was
out to see the country, the waterfalls, the wildlife, not to set a record."
Espy was the second person to walk the entire
A.T. in one stretch. Doug Wilcox, in shorts (opposite), gives
the Reverend Bill E. Hinton a note expressing the gratitude of thousands
of hikers who have found welcome comfort at The Place.

FOLLOWING PAGES: Viewed south from Three Ridges, the A.T.
descends into the Tye River Valley and climbs the 4,063 feet of The Priest,
in Virginia's George Washington National Forest.
MIKE WARREN

(Continued from page 51) booze, women, and salt," he confided to me. "Not necessarily in that order." He nudged me with an elbow and laughed: "Miss salt the most."

We made a couple of big X's with two-by-sixes and set them astride the fence, then nailed steps to them. One of the X's rested against a young oak tree, which gave the stile added support. It sounds simple—and was, actually—but it occupied us for most of the day. We took our time and did a proper job. Andy was lavish with compliments. If I managed to cut a chunk off a two-by-six without hurting myself, he would say, "Nice job, nice job!" And he was exuberant in his praise of our work. "Beautiful, beautiful," he would murmur. "This is going to be the most beautiful stile that was ever built."

Farmers were making hay in an adjacent field, and we could hear them down there as we worked: their shouts, their engines, their dog barking. The stile turned out just fine, a sturdy and handsome piece of work. "What did I tell you?" said Andy. "This is without doubt the finest stile in the state of Virginia." So, hikers: When you're hiking north through Virginia near the trail crossing of Route 42 and you climb a gentle hill through a pasture and reach a fence along the ridgeline with the finest stile in the state straddling it, before you step up on that bottom rung, wipe your feet.

I ran into Andy again about a month later when I returned to Virginia, to the campus of Lynchburg College, in Lynchburg, for the week-long biennial meeting—the 26th—of the Appalachian Trail Conference. Members of the ATC gather every other year at a location near the trail. This year about a thousand had registered.

A t the opening session, speeches were the order of the day. We were welcomed and greeted by several speakers, then given a keynote address by Patrick F. Noonan, president of the Conservation Fund. He told us, among other things, that conservation groups are being formed at an estimated rate of 400 a year; that we represented conservation at its finest; that the Park Service had acquired 1,600 parcels of A.T. land in nine years—one every two days, "an incredible accomplishment"; and that the country needs a national endowment for outdoor recreation similar to the National Endowments for the Arts and for the Humanities.

Dave Richie, formerly of the Park Service and for years a familiar presence on the trail and at trail functions, reported that fewer than 200 miles of A.T. remain unprotected and predicted the job would be finished by 1991.

Tom Lennon, national trail coordinator of the Forest Service, confessed to being the same age as the trail and also to having proposed to his wife 30 years earlier during a hike on the Appalachian Trail. Of the 842 miles of the trail on Forest Service land, he told us, fewer than 9 miles remain unprotected. "Those 9 miles, though," he said, "are the toughest nuts to crack."

The general business meeting began a couple of days later, with greetings from Ray Hunt, a treasurer's report (assets of $1,468,871, ten times liabilities), instructions on how to vote, and the election of a new board of managers. Twenty-four nominees trooped to the front of the

TULIP TREE *(Liriodendron tulipifera)*

room and stood, like a chorus line, while we voted on them as a unit.

The resolutions committee presented resolutions supporting the federal Land and Water Conservation Fund and thanking the conference committee for its work. Another called for the ATC logo to read "from Georgia to Maine"—since that's the direction nearly all thru-hikers walk—instead of "from Maine to Georgia." This resolution is traditionally introduced by Southerners at almost every meeting, I was told, and is always defeated, as it was again. Another resolution, a rather complicated one, had to do with the mechanism whereby ATC members could "input" their management ideas into the ATC's organization. Defeated, despite applause. The final resolution called on the ATC to concentrate on the *soul* of the trail, as opposed to its body. This caused some puzzlement and discussion. "Isn't it the soul of an organization that keeps the body together?" a woman asked. Passed.

The meeting concluded, and the trail beckoned northward. Between Lynchburg and Shenandoah National Park, the A.T. runs almost entirely within George Washington National Forest. North of Salt Log Gap, Spy Rock provides fine panoramic views on clear days of the Valley of Virginia to the west. Farther north, at the Tye River, a suspension bridge bobs and sways as it carries hikers above a 60-foot-wide stream.

The trail passes into Shenandoah National Park north of Rockfish Gap and stays there for the next 95 miles. The 300 square miles the park encompasses is land that has felt the heavy hand of man in the past but is now beautifully recovered. To wander through these mountains, you would hardly suspect that just 70 years ago much of this area was denuded, farming and grazing having removed virtually every vestige of forest. Old photographs show these hills as bare of trees as a Kansas pasture. So in the twenties when the Park Service was looking for a suitable area for an Appalachian park, the roughly 70 miles of ridgeline between Waynesboro and Front Royal looked ideal. President Coolidge signed legislation authorizing the establishment of park boundaries in 1925, and money from the Commonwealth of Virginia and from private donations paid for the 176,429 acres that were deeded to the federal government in December 1935. President Roosevelt came to the park on July 3, 1936, to dedicate it.

Even before the establishment of the park, as early as the turn of the century, families had been moving out of the area. The blight that killed the chestnut trees, once one of the area's most plentiful species, seemed to serve as a final blow. Still, some 450 families residing in the park were forced to move. In all, 3,870 private tracts of land were acquired. The old farms soon were overgrown with shrubs, locusts, and pines, which in turn have been replaced by the oak, hickory, and other species of a mature deciduous forest.

Between 1933 and 1942, the CCC built 13,100 miles of hiking trails in this country, including many of the 500 miles of trails in Shenandoah Park. It was a remarkable federal program, this gathering up of unemployed young men, shipping them off to camps in the countryside, and putting them to work building many of the parks and recreation facilities still enjoyed today. They were treated as soldiers and paid a wage that, although minimal, helped put them and their families back on their economic feet. For many, it was the time of their lives, and survivors still gather for nostalgic reunions.

Cecil Weaver, now 74, was a 19-year-old from nearby Luray when he joined up in 1933. Until recently, he worked for the park in its maintenance division. One of the projects he helped on back in the thirties was clearing the section of the Appalachian Trail that runs within 200 yards of the Elkwallow Picnic Area. I met Cecil there and got him to stroll a ways on the trail and to reminisce about his experiences half a century earlier in the CCC.

"I was up here $4\frac{1}{2}$ years," he told me. "An enlistment was for 6 months, but you could reenlist if you wanted. They had us in tents down by Sperryville, but then they moved us up here—just over that hill—and built barracks. Four barracks and a mess hall. Food was good. Lots of chicken.

"This was all pasture then. Now it's all grown up. I did a little of everything—cleared trail, worked on Skyline Drive. Work was hard. We cleared lots of dead timber, big hollow chestnut trees. Some of 'em had squirrels in 'em, some had honeybees. Got stung on the tongue once, eating honey.

"We tore down lots of houses. Some nice houses in here we took down. One fella didn't want to move out. They put him in jail, and we went in there and got all his house furniture and took it to Luray and stored it. We took that house down too, took 'em *all* down."

He reached up and gently caressed a tree that had an A.T. blaze on it. "Made good money—a dollar a day. On weekends, we'd go down to Luray or Front Royal, a big truck of us, maybe 25 or 30 boys. We *owned* those towns. After a while, people would come up in their old cars to see the park. We'd be up on the bank, workin', and there'd be these girls in the cars. I remember them, those girls, wavin' and hollerin'. Oh, we had a time, buddy...."

Nearby Big Meadows is a favorite place of mine in the Shenandoah—and dawn is a favorite time. The deer then are as thick as rabbits—and as playful. They dash across the meadow with a rocking-horse motion, their white tails flashing. The dew makes the blueberry bushes glisten and patterns the Queen Anne's lace. Goldfinches perch in scraggly trees and take flight in their roller-coaster swoops. Big Meadows, the largest open area in the park, is one of those places that would soon become forest if left alone, so the Park Service mows and burns it every couple of years.

It is true that man's heavy hand has brought changes to the mountains in this park, and now nature is poised to bring about another kind of change: The gypsy moth has crossed the northern border of the park and is moving south. In the northern third, I saw a lot of denuded trees.

The first gypsy moths in the U.S. escaped from a biologist's laboratory in Massachusetts in 1869. They have been spreading, mostly southward, ever since. They were first found in the park in 1983, and the Park Service concedes that defoliation will occur and trees will die, for 85 percent of the trees in the park are species preferred by gypsy moths. There is no way to eliminate them, but some methods help to control the voracious little creatures. Spraying has been tried. Lure tapes attached to trees at mating time confuse some of the males. And scraping egg masses from trees and vehicles has slightly slowed their spread.

Trying to find a bright side to look on, park officials point out that change has been a constant force in the Blue Ridge Mountains since time began. The relatively recent loss of the chestnut trees, for instance, was a traumatic alteration of the biota. So the damage done by gypsy moths can be viewed as simply another step in an ongoing process of death and rejuvenation. The new forest will be different from the old, but there's no reason to suppose that it will be less magnificent. Still, while the change is taking place, the dead and dying trees are a piteous sight.

North of the park, paralleling the Shenandoah River, the trail butts up against the Conservation and Research Center of the Smithsonian Institution's National Zoological Park. The government has owned this property since 1911, when the Army began using it as a remount station for the cavalry. During World War II, German POWs were housed here, but since 1974 the zoo has used it as a place to research and breed some of the world's endangered animals—mostly mammals and birds.

I stopped by the headquarters, where I found Jack Williams, facility manager. He agreed to show me around, but only if anything I wrote began, "Although closed to the general public. . . ."

"But Jack. . . ."

Courteously but firmly Jack said: "If a hiker shows up here, he's directed back to the highway, the same way he came in. I'm sorry, but we have no facilities for the public. There are extremely rare animals here, many of them shy and delicate. We can't risk having them disturbed."

The trail runs along the edge of the property for a mile and a half, and a hiker, if he's lucky, might see some pretty exotic creatures peering at him through the fence as he walks by. I hiked with Jack for a bit along the A.T., with zebras grazing on a hillside and, near a hay barn, an onager shyly watching us go by. It looked like a cream-colored donkey. The fences are double, so the animals and hikers can't get too close to each other. Double fences also make it twice as hard for one of these rare creatures to escape, or for local deer, which sometimes perceive the grass inside as greener, to get in.

Near the fence was a sign, "Entering Restricted Grounds. Breeding Center, National Zoological Park. Pets on Leash. No Camping. No Fires. Stay on Trail. Violators Will Be Eaten." ☐

ALLEGHENY SERVICEBERRY *(Amelanchier laevis)*

CHRIS JOHNS (BOTH)

City lights of Waynesboro, Virginia, glitter far below
as thru-hiker Jerry Gramling, Jr., beds down on Little Calf
Mountain. High pastureland at nearly 3,000 feet
offers some of the most sweeping views found along the trail.
Jerry's nylon tent and other lightweight gear
honor the A.T. axiom: "First, last, and always, travel light."

Sharp-eyed hunter,
a screech owl
clutches its meal,
a white-footed mouse.
Night transforms
the trail. The day's hazy
air cools and clears.
Moonlight tones
the woods. Frogs belt
out marsh songs
a cappella. Insects chirr
violinlike, and
from somewhere this
side of the full moon
comes the owl's
solo—more of an eerie,
quavering whistle
than a screech.

FRED J. ALSOP III

Luminescent softness of dawn lures a whitetail
doe out of the woods to graze at Big Meadows. Accessible from
Skyline Drive, this island of grasses and shrubs
in a sea of forest occupies 200 acres on the crest of the
Blue Ridge Mountains in Virginia's Shenandoah National Park.
In this high meadow, hundreds of varieties
of animals and plants thrive year-round.

FOLLOWING PAGES: Mountain laurel, maple-leaved viburnum, and table-mountain pine landscape massive slabs of granite, the billion-year-old core rock of the Blue Ridge. Winding through Shenandoah National Park, the A.T. leads to misty peaks, sunny clearings, shady hollows, and rocky havens.

© DAVID MUENCH 1988

*Small-scale splendor: Columbine blossoms
nod beside a shelf of lichen-blazed greenstone, and
a tiger swallowtail collects nectar from a pasture
thistle. To ensure access to such vignettes of natural
wonder, an army of volunteers keeps
the trail in repair. The task may rank as
the world's largest volunteer effort in support
of a recreational facility.*

© DAVID MUENCH 1988

The Trail's
Rocky Heart

On the lawn of the Appalachian Trail Conference headquarters, in Harpers Ferry, West Virginia, I overheard two tough-looking thru-hikers talking. "... a black raspberry milk shake that was *almost pure ice cream*," one of them was saying. It's the sort of thing thru-hikers talk about. In *The Philosopher's Guide,* a book of tips for thru-hikers, the acronym AYCE ("ace")—All You Can Eat—is the highest accolade a restaurant or hostel can receive.

Harpers Ferry is an appropriate historic site for the headquarters of the Appalachian Trail Conference. A short relocation in 1986 brought the trail back into town, where it passes among the old buildings of the Harpers Ferry National Historical Park. It was at the U.S. Armory here that fiery John Brown staged his bloody preview to the Civil War.

Too, the town is about halfway between Maine and Georgia, though the precise midpoint of the trail lies some 75 miles north, in Pennsylvania. The ATC headquarters is in an old commercial building on a tree-shaded corner of Washington and Jackson Streets, a few blocks up the hill from the historical park's downtown district.

The first person you meet inside the front door is Jean Cashin, a legendary figure among hikers. The ATC calls her an "information specialist," and certainly she is that. Phone the ATC with a question, and it is likely Jean who will have the answer. But she is much more. A grandmotherly figure—in fact, a grandmother—she greets visitors and hikers with friendliness, courtesy, and curiosity. If they're thru-hikers, she takes a snapshot of them on the front steps of the headquarters and inserts it in thick albums she maintains.

She is the supervisor of the headquarters' numerous volunteers; oversees the operation of a sales desk that dispenses guidebooks, maps, and T-shirts; watches over cluttered archives and memorabilia that include

Atop Weverton Cliffs, in Maryland, just off
the Appalachian Trail, day-hikers Libby and Bill Howard
catch their breath above the Potomac River gorge.
Above: A rock near the trail in Pennsylvania
features the A.T. symbol painted in white.
CHRIS JOHNS (ABOVE)

Benton MacKaye's bedroll and pack. In 1987 Jean and the volunteers responded to more than 40,000 requests for information about the trail.

In a column in the *Appalachian Trailway News* called "Up Front," she writes about her days. She gets a lot of mail from children. One little boy asked her to send him the Appalachian Trail, and another, from Texas, wrote: "I have been to the Appalachian Scenic Trail before, and I think it is a great park. I especially love the way you talk there."

One of the recent photos in Jean's album was of Jerry Gramling, whose parents Sam and I had met in the snows of Georgia. I had been seeing his trail name—Lido Bandito—in registers along the trail, but he had always been ahead of me. I called his parents to see how he was doing.

He was doing just fine, I was told. They had been in touch with him several times, had even joined him once or twice, driving all night for brief weekend visits. They were getting so much vicarious enjoyment from his hike that they had begun to talk about walking the trail themselves, after retirement. "Right *now* it appeals to me," said his mother. "We'll see."

She had taken a large map of the A.T. to her office and there kept track of Jerry's progress on it with a colored pin. Co-workers were interested and supportive. "But it doesn't help to have people say, 'Don't you *worry* about him?' Of course I worry about him, but he wanted to do this so badly."

The Appalachian Trail Project Office of the National Park Service is also located in Harpers Ferry. Over the years, the cooperation between the two has been informal and easy—yet crucial to the lasting success of the trail. Early on, it became apparent to the Park Service that the trail would need a special kind of management. Linear parkland averaging a thousand feet in width cannot be run the same way as Yosemite, say, or Yellowstone. So in 1984 the Park Service and the ATC signed a landmark cooperative agreement, made possible by Section 7(h) of the National Trails System Act of 1968, as amended. It delegates to the ATC official responsibility for managing the trail on Park Service land in 8 of the 14 trail states. Eventually some 98,000 acres of federal land and 600 miles of the Appalachian Trail will come under ATC management. The ATC, in turn, delegates day-to-day responsibility to the volunteers in local clubs.

It is a unique situation, the first time the Park Service has turned over land management responsibility of this magnitude to private citizens. Ruth Blackburn, ATC chairman emeritus, said, "With the delegation of responsibility to ATC, and then to the clubs, we have completed a cycle.... Once again, it is up to the volunteers." William P. Clark, then Secretary of the Interior, called the agreement "a model of cooperation and goodwill" between the federal government and citizens. Perhaps the person most responsible for guiding the agreement through the bureaucratic thickets was Dave Richie, then head of the Park Service's Appalachian Trail Project Office. "Volunteers really want to do the work," he said. "They are far more numerous and better distributed along the trail than government employees are ever likely to be."

The trail in Harpers Ferry does not pass directly by the headquarters; a

AMERICAN SYCAMORE *(Platanus occidentalis)*

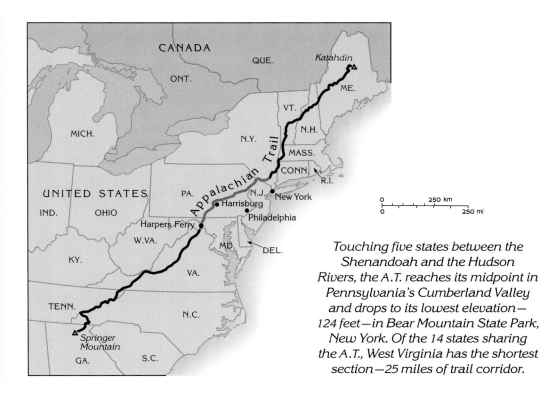

Touching five states between the Shenandoah and the Hudson Rivers, the A.T. reaches its midpoint in Pennsylvania's Cumberland Valley and drops to its lowest elevation— 124 feet—in Bear Mountain State Park, New York. Of the 14 states sharing the A.T., West Virginia has the shortest section—25 miles of trail corridor.

blue-blazed side trail leads hikers a quarter of a mile to it. The A.T. itself edges along a wooded bluff as it enters town, passing the cemetery where Robert Harper, whose ferry gave the town its name, is buried. Eroded headstones tilt in the sun there, and cottontails bob through the long grass.

Proceeding past the famous Jefferson Rock, the trail descends toward the center of town on old stone steps, passing the house built by Robert Harper between 1775 and 1782—the oldest surviving structure in the park. Near the foot of the steps, among the historic buildings, is the Visitor Center. Outside it, on the summer day I passed through, fretful tourists stunned by the heat and the sun were whacking their fractious children. Skirting Arsenal Square and John Brown's Fort, the A.T. enters Maryland as it crosses the Potomac River on a footbridge built especially for it in 1986, cantilevered from the 1894 Baltimore and Ohio Railroad Bridge. A level, quiet stretch of trail runs along the Chesapeake and Ohio Canal towpath for 2.8 miles. Then it enters the forest and climbs on switchbacks to Weverton Cliffs, pauses for a last look back—a great blue heron fishing in the shallows of the Shenandoah, a flock of Canada geese rising from the water.

Between Harpers Ferry and the Hudson River, a stretch of some 380 miles, the trail meanders through mostly hardwood forest on old, stoopshouldered mountains and ridges. The valleys below flatten into farmland. The Potomac and the Susquehanna are the big rivers, but their modern counterparts—Interstates 80 and 81—are more of a presence to hikers.

Harrisburg, in Pennsylvania, is a sprawling city near the trail. Farther north the bright lights of New York City pulse at night on the horizon.

Forty miles of the trail lie in Maryland, most of them along the summit of South Mountain. Shaped like a loaf of French bread, the mountain played an important role in one of the battles of the Civil War. With General Lee's Confederate army in three scattered pieces, General McClellan tried to get his Union forces through the gaps of South Mountain to attack and destroy Lee's army one piece at a time. McClellan might have succeeded, but he dawdled. Lee slowed him at the gaps, got his army reassembled, and they fought a major battle at nearby Antietam Creek three days later. So as a hiker walks along South Mountain and dips into its gaps, the Civil War is a constantly recurring presence.

One of the people killed during the Battle of South Mountain was Maj. Gen. Jesse L. Reno, commander of the Union left flank. A monument dedicated to him is a few steps from the trail about six miles north of Gathland State Park. On the back of the granite monument are inscribed the general's battles: Vera Cruz, Cerro Cordo, Contreras, Churubusco, Chapultepec, Roanoke Island, New Berne, Camden, Bull Run, Chantilly, and South Mountain.

I walked from Gathland back toward Harpers Ferry one evening, a seven-mile stroll on the A.T. sponsored by the Maryland Forest, Park and Wildlife Service. Among the 40 or so walkers was, by chance, Jean Roesser, a member of the Maryland House of Delegates and at that time a member of ANSTAC—the Appalachian National Scenic Trail Advisory Council. ANSTAC, a board of 35 members from up and down the trail, serves as a forum for trail interests, as well as a sounding board for new management ideas. Jean was enjoying her stroll, only the third time she had been on the A.T. "But I've made up my mind," she told me, as we walked along through the late afternoon, "I'm going to hike all 40 miles here in Maryland."

I asked Jean about her association with ANSTAC. "Like all the members, I was appointed by the secretary of the interior, and I'm serving a second two-year term," she said. "One of our jobs is to advise the secretary on land acquisition for the trail. We still have more than eight miles yet to protect here in Maryland. We've got to get it locked up. It's been a loose end too long."

Later, hiking northward toward Annapolis Rocks, I met a man with what many people might call the perfect summer job: College student Dwayne Ericson was working as a trail runner. It was his job to walk the Appalachian Trail in Maryland all summer long. A picture of calm authority in his beige shirt and shorts, Dwayne reported: "I'm mostly a public relations person. I answer questions, and if I see visitors breaking a rule I advise them of it." Dwayne checks on the shelters and campsites in the Maryland section, looking for litter and abuse and overuse. At Annapolis Rocks we sat in the sun, gazing westward across the rolling Maryland countryside.

Just before crossing the state line into Pennsylvania, the trail moseys through Pen Mar County Park, once the site of one of the most famous

PITCH PINE *(Pinus rigida)*

resorts in the East. In the 1870s the Western Maryland Railroad built an amusement park here as a destination for its excursion trains. The Lutherans once assembled a flock of 15,000 here for a picnic.

Pennsylvania sometimes gets a bad rap from backpackers. It's a long state, in trail terms—230 miles. Its mountains are very like hills, seldom more than 1,200 feet above the valleys. Worse, the Ice Age left in Pennsylvania a shattered mass of jagged rocks that make for very difficult walking. And if you traced the route of the trail on a highway map, you might think it impossible for a footpath to negotiate such a citified state without being constantly in someone's suburbs. But there are pluses to be found in Pennsylvania. Much of the trail runs through what the guidebook calls "pleasing woods," and at practically every turn is another remnant of Pennsylvania's long and storied past, or a Pennsylvanian eager to be hospitable, or a rocky outcrop warmed by the sun to the perfect temperature for a nap.

South-central Pennsylvania was once the heart of a busy charcoal iron industry, active from about 1740 until the end of the 19th century. At hearths wood was burned to produce the charcoal that fired the iron furnaces. The round, flat areas sprinkled throughout the forests are the remnants of those hearths. In Caledonia State Park the trail passes a model of a relatively short-lived iron furnace that was put into operation in 1837 and destroyed by Confederate troops on their way to Gettysburg in 1863. At the park's swimming pool, closed this weekday morning, a kingfisher perched on the lifeguard's chair and made occasional swooping forays to the creek. The top of its head bristled with a spiky crest, like a punk rocker's hair. Nearby, robins plucked bugs from tall grass, and a crow sounded a raucous alarm from a treetop.

Pine Grove Furnace also has its own state park. At a camp store there I watched two hikers shopping. They bought loaves of bread, a jar of peanut butter, a jar of jelly, two boxes of Pop-Tarts, a carton of Twinkies, a box of cookies, some Lipton instant soup, and toilet paper. Then they sat on the front porch of the store and ate the Twinkies. *All* of them. They were among the few southbound thru-hikers I had met. They expected to finish at Springer Mountain in about three more months.

As it exits Pine Grove Furnace State Park, the A.T. climbs Piney Mountain and intersects a blue-blazed side trail that leads half a mile to Pole Steeple overlook. The sound of shouting lured me there, where I found 2 counselors and 14 teenagers. They were attending a month-long adventure camp nearby—hiking, bicycling, rafting—and had come to Pole Steeple for a day of rock climbing. From the top I could see the park's Laurel Lake far below. Lilliputian people in toy boats made fading V's there on its still waters.

Another lake, much smaller, is at the center of an ATC success story about 20 miles north, in Boiling Springs, near where the trail begins its crossing of Cumberland Valley. "Springs" is hardly the word for this body of water in the middle of town. Dozens of bubbling founts combine to create a lake the size of a city block. Ducks and geese patrol its surface, begging handouts from children, and willows weep on its shores.

By chance I met Dave Startzell, executive director of the ATC, there one day, the very day the ATC announced the agreement to purchase the lake and some adjacent property. "The conference has been interested in

85

preserving these properties for several years," Dave told me. "Recently, though, when developers began surveying the lake's eastern shore for a townhouse development, the town mobilized itself and solicited donations—several of them sizable—from local citizens and organizations. These donations enabled the ATC's Trust for Appalachian Trail Lands to make the purchase." The trust uses private contributions to acquire unprotected land, then usually turns it over to the public. It has assisted in the protection of more than 7,000 acres since 1982. "The trust will sell the lake to the Pennsylvania Fish Commission," Dave explained, "and the land to the National Park Service at or below our actual cost."

The trail will be rerouted through town so backpackers will have access to stores, a restaurant, a post office, a swimming pool, fishing, even a bed and breakfast establishment. And, most important, the trail will run along the edge of one of the most beautiful lakes in Pennsylvania. At the transfer ceremony, Craig Dunn, former chairman of the trust's advisory committee, said, "I believe the village of Boiling Springs will become one of the jewels in the memories of those who hike the Appalachian Trail." I believe he's right.

Boiling Springs sits at the southern edge of the broad and congested Cumberland Valley. The guidebook gives fair warning: "The valley is mostly residential along the route of the Trail and few commercial businesses are passed. There is little shade in the valley and summer hiking can be hot and dry. CARRY WATER. Beware of dogs."

I came down out of the woods, heading north, and found myself on a blacktop highway, passing through woods, then cornfields. I crossed Yellow Breeches Creek, where there's a sign: No Parking at Any Time. Here on the macadam, I noted, there's a yellow line down the middle of the Appalachian Trail. Beyond Churchtown, a village of small brick houses with pickups in most driveways, were cornfields and barns and a sign: Slow—Cattle Crossing. From the evidence, some had recently crossed. Soon there were suburbs on my left and another sign, for a bridge: Weight Limit 15 Tons. Sometimes it feels as if that's about what your pack weighs. I crossed above the Pennsylvania Turnpike on an old concrete bridge and, in a bit, turned right on the Harrisburg Pike, Route 11. Cars, trucks, and buses slapped at me with their tail winds. I turned left at a Hess station, crossed over Interstate 81, passed through more farms and suburbs, and headed uphill on Deer Lane. In woods now, in a driveway on Ridge Road, was my last sight of civilization: a black Chrysler LeBaron. As I continued up a road fit only for jeeps and walkers, the Cumberland Valley was finally behind me.

Boiling Springs is a key component of a new route across the Cumberland Valley, a route that was not easy to agree upon. Many landowners opposed putting the trail on the valley's only high ground—a ridge running north and south nearly across it. But this "ridge route" is largely wooded and was the route-of-choice of most hikers and of the ATC. The landowners formed Citizens Against the New Trail (CANT) to oppose the route. After years of public meetings, open houses, opinion surveys, and environmental assessments, the Park Service in 1985 approved the ridge route and began acquiring the land. Since then, former CANT members have worked jointly with the Cumberland Valley A.T. Management Committee. So the 14 miles of unprotected trail in the Cumberland Valley—one of the longest segments still vulnerable to development—will soon be protected.

Ray Hunt, representing the ATC, has written: "The new Trail location should be a tremendous improvement in the footway and its surroundings . . . a rich mixture of woods on low ridges, farmland, and small communities. The Trail will be safer, no longer being on heavily traveled paved roads. Trail continuity will be preserved . . . , [and] I hope that, in time, the community will come to see these values more than it does now."

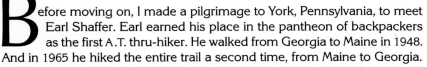

Before moving on, I made a pilgrimage to York, Pennsylvania, to meet Earl Shaffer. Earl earned his place in the pantheon of backpackers as the first A.T. thru-hiker. He walked from Georgia to Maine in 1948. And in 1965 he hiked the entire trail a second time, from Maine to Georgia.

He grew up here in southern Pennsylvania, hunting and fishing with brothers and friends. One friend, especially, named Walter, shared Earl's love of the woods. "Walter's the one who told me about the Appalachian Trail," Earl said. "In 1937, my younger brother, Evan, and I went for a hike on the A.T., for a week. We arranged for our older brother, Dan, to pick us up in seven days, but we didn't have any idea how long the hike was going to take. It was in summer, and we'd get up at first light and start hiking, hike all day. In two days' time we were there." He laughed. "Had a five-day wait, in the rain. We had a tent whose roof leaked but whose floor didn't, so we sat in a pool of water. Then we ran out of food, so we went down to this little town. I had tried to shave with a straight razor and no mirror and had myself all cut up. People in town were scared to death of us."

Fit and muscular at 68, Earl sat on a sofa sipping coffee and remembering, in a shy voice, his early life. He and Walter went off to World War II in the early forties, to separate parts of the Pacific. "We had that ESP," he said softly. "I *knew* when he was killed." He died on Iwo Jima with the Marines.

Confused and depressed when peace came—"I was in the war too long"—Earl in his late 20s set off to walk the Appalachian Trail. He began in April—"The true first month of the year." Equipment was primitive by today's standards. He modified an old Army rucksack and in it carried a blanket, a cook kit, clothing, poncho, rain hat, and food. The trail was rough and marked haphazardly then, and often he was lost. "Sometimes I'd go a day or two and maybe see one blaze." He would come down out of the hills to ask directions, but many locals had never heard of *(Continued on page 104)*

FOLLOWING PAGES: Glowing at daybreak beyond the shaley cliffs of Maryland Heights, Harpers Ferry, West Virginia, nestles at the confluence of the Shenandoah River, left, and the Potomac, lower right. Foot travelers passing through town on the A.T. find a hearty welcome at the Appalachian Trail Conference headquarters, located here.

EASTERN REDBUD *(Cercis canadensis)*

MIKE WARREN

Outside Pine Knob Shelter (opposite)
on South Mountain in Maryland Ron Fisher, left,
greets trail runner Dwayne Ericson.
All along the A.T., overnight shelters provide
protection from the elements. Unlike
hikers, blue flag iris (above) thrives on dampness.

FOLLOWING PAGES: Sunlight filters
through hemlock and white pine in a swampy
corner of Pine Grove Furnace State Park, in
Pennsylvania. The A.T. passes right by
the iron furnace that gave the park its name.

*Eyes on the path, Dave Crosby, his son, Chris, and their
dog, Bandit, negotiate a section of the A.T. in central Pennsylvania
famous for its rockiness. Chris wields a hickory and
aluminum staff made by his father. Below, the trio from Reading
cools out at Northkill Creek, a short distance off the A.T.*

FOLLOWING PAGES: *Knee-deep in Yellow Breeches Creek,
in Pennsylvania, a flycaster waits at dusk for the sudden strike of
a trout. The A.T. crosses this prime trout fishing
stream, fed by cold waters from Boiling Springs Lake.*

CHRIS JOHNS (BOTH AND OVERLEAF)

*Shelter designer Dave Crosby,
scribing logs (above), and other members of the
Blue Mountain Eagle Climbing Club built
a shelter miles from its permanent location on the
A.T. in Pennsylvania. As part of a training
mission, the Pennsylvania Army National Guard
flew the seven-ton structure (right) to the trail.
After set-down, Chuck Wood, in patchwork jacket,
and Todd Gladfelter (top) remove the bracing.*

CHRIS JOHNS (ABOVE AND UPPER LEFT)

*Trail of fog hugs
the Delaware River. The
A.T. passes through
the Delaware Water Gap
as it moves from
Pennsylvania into
New Jersey, where it follows
Kittatinny Ridge. At
Bear Mountain State Park,
a statue of the poet
Walt Whitman greets
hikers. Chiseled in
granite nearby are lines
from his paean
to traveling, "Song of
the Open Road."*

Getaways and get-togethers coincide on the A.T.
as it nears the Hudson River. Fathers with young children
socialize on a paved portion (above) in
Bear Mountain State Park, a weekend magnet for
residents of New York City. In adjoining
Harriman State Park, trail veteran Dave Sherman,
a 2,000-miler, opts for serious hiking as he tackles a passage
called the Lemon Squeezer (left).

(Continued from page 87) the Appalachian Trail. "But no matter how lost I got, I always managed to go a few miles in the right direction." His morale hit bottom in Connecticut after a long period of steady rain. "In the pathways of sadness," my old hymnal tells me, "Sweetest lilies may grow." He said that at night whippoorwills came so close to his fire their eyes reflected red and that once he was kept awake by the ominous sound of millions of inchworms munching tree foliage overhead. Coming upon a stretch of trail with wire strung alongside it on poles, he met a blind man making his way there. One night Earl dreamed that the path moved like a treadmill, and he was losing ground. Another time he counted steps and calculated his own at better than two thousand to a mile, or about five million from Georgia to Maine.

He finished the trail on August 5, taught himself the art of writing, and produced *Walking With Spring,* to me one of the most observant and thoughtful books ever written about the Appalachian Trail.

I left him hatching plans for extending the A.T. Run a trail west from Katahdin, he says, to hook up again with Vermont's Long Trail. Bring it south through the Adirondacks and the Alleghenies to Springer Mountain and thus make of the Appalachian Trail a 5,000-mile-long loop, a truly endless trail. It's the sort of vision that I think would have appealed to Benton MacKaye.

And I found another vision of Benton MacKaye's—the army of volunteers—stronger than ever. On Peters Mountain, across the Susquehanna River from Duncannon, I joined a crew as they did some work around a shelter. A woman was painting its floor, several men were making a trail from it to the site of a new privy, and others were digging a hole for the privy. Dennis Shaffer, then mid-Atlantic regional representative of the ATC, was there. "Even here, deep in the woods, we have to abide by local regulations," he told me. "The site for the privy was selected by the township sewage officer, and the building permit cost us $22."

Down the slope, other volunteers were improving the spring, making a deeper pool where the water poured from a pipe. A husky young man named Ken found a crayfish in the work area, in danger of being trampled into the mud. He picked it up gently in his thick gloves and carried it a few yards downstream, out of harm's way.

These volunteers—the Keystone Trail Crew, now called the Mid-Atlantic Crew—were part of an ATC program to train people to work on the A.T. and also to assist local clubs with maintenance projects. The first such group, begun in Virginia in 1983, was the Konnarock Crew. People could sign up for a few days of labor, or a few months. They were fed, sheltered, and put to work. In 1984 the Keystone group was organized here in Pennsylvania.

In 1987 the Konnarock Crew cleared or constructed 25,000 feet of trail, built 140 steps and 40 water bars, put up 4 bridges, and built 1 shelter and upgraded 2 others. The Keystone Crew did similar work. Together, they volunteered more than 7,000 hours of labor. Crew programs are planned for New York, New Jersey, Vermont, and New Hampshire. The Maine Appalachian Trail Club is assisted each summer by volunteers from the Student

CHESTNUT OAK *(Quercus prinus)*

Conservation Association. In 1987, some 3,680 men and women from the crews and the ATC's 31 maintaining clubs labored 105,700 hours on the A.T.

Until the ATC was given formal responsibility for trail management, the work of volunteers stopped with maintaining the path itself, with blazing the trail, and with erecting shelters, bridges, and signs. But now volunteers check for easement violations, timber theft, dumping, and any other abuses.

Volunteers do more: They stop by headquarters in Harpers Ferry to give Jean Cashin a hand with addressing envelopes or answering phones; they attend meetings, often miles from home; they send letters and make phone calls to local and national politicians and officials; they visit worried landowners to explain the concept of the trail; they write and produce some of the guidebooks; lawyers volunteer legal services; and those interested in history work on the ATC's history and records committee.

It is difficult to calculate how many millions of dollars this volunteer labor saves the Park and Forest Services each year, a saving not lost on a financially strapped federal government. Indeed, some resource managers deplore efforts to decrease funding for professional staffs and rely on volunteers instead. No volunteer, they say, no matter how eager, can replace a full-time biologist, for instance. The ATC takes care to call on professional help when needed, and many of its volunteers are resource-related professionals.

But, back on the trail. . . . The plaque on the old Waterville Bridge, which now carries the A.T. across Swatara Creek, reads, "1890. Built by the Berlin Iron Bridge Co., East Berlin, Conn." Its graceful gray trusses made me think of a child's erector set. Downstream, a man and a woman with a big black dog were picnicking on the bank. Farther on, I passed under bridges of a very different sort: the Interstate 81 highway bridges. It's dusty and bare underneath, for little water or sunlight penetrates here. A few feet overhead, the bridges squeak and thunder as traffic roars across. It seemed unnatural and faintly illicit to be on the wrong side of a bridge. I half expected someone to come along and order me topside.

I remember arriving in Port Clinton. I crossed the Schuylkill River on a rusty railroad bridge and looked down in time to see a fisherman catch something. As I walked through town, women were hanging out wash. A cat was asleep in a window, whiskers twitching.

I found Grace A. Sunday in her peanut shop, beneath a sign of two elephants holding a peanut. Inside were dozens of jars of different kinds of candy and peanuts. Grace roasts her own nuts and makes her own caramel corn, peanut clusters, candy, and peanut butter. I asked her how she kept her figure. "I don't eat the stuff," she said. "Stand over it all day, you lose your appetite." A neighbor's toy terrier came to the door, barked, was let in, sat in front of a fan in the corner, panted, sat some more, went to the door, barked, was let out. Grace offered me a sample of her potato candy. It looked like an ice-cream-cake roll and tasted like peanut butter pie. Delicious.

I remember the rocks of Pennsylvania getting, if anything, sharper and meaner until, in places, they seemed diabolical. You pick your steps carefully, and the jagged rocks do their best to twist your ankles or de-sole your boots. As I paused for lunch and the view at Wolf Rocks, a pileated woodpecker flew over my head out over the valley. Its wingbeats were strong but irregular, as if each stroke required a moment's thought. Back in the mid-seventies, developers had plans for a huge community here, more than 700 half-acre lots that would have covered the ridge and buried the A.T. in houses. An access road would have ended at the overlook, but the view would have been of rooftops and driveways. The townships and the county commissioners approved the plans, but citizen opposition slowed the effort, and federal and state acquisition brought the project to a halt.

Another overlook, on down the trail, gave me a view into the valley. Looking down from such a ridge, a backpacker is struck by the contrast between the snail's pace of his own life and the frantic pace of others'. A hawk went by at eye level and circled lazily as I ate my apple. Like a bird itself, I thought, the Appalachian Trail is often up here where the hawks are.

People sometimes wonder if the A.T. is safe. I felt fear only once—as I crossed the Delaware River on the Interstate 80 bridge at Delaware Water Gap to enter New Jersey. You walk a narrow sidewalk, your hand sliding along a railing, and by the time you reach the middle, trucks are roaring past two feet from your shoulder. Grit and gravel fly. The noise is fierce, and blasts of wind threaten to topple you off into the water. The bridge *moves;* you feel it rise and fall. You realize you are wide-eyed with terror, and you're clutching the handrail with a sweaty palm. It makes a dramatic end to Pennsylvania.

Perhaps nowhere in American geography can you see so clearly the battle waged between water and mountains as at the Delaware Water Gap, a textbook illustration of the slow but steady force of moving water. During millions of years, the Delaware River system cut through Kittatinny Ridge, helping create today's landscape. In 1962 Congress authorized a dam across the Delaware, and land that would have been flooded was acquired by the federal government. But opposition has endlessly postponed the dam, now unlikely ever to be built. So the area has been designated the Delaware Water Gap National Recreation Area. It straddles the river for some 35 miles, and the A.T. runs through it on Kittatinny Ridge for 25 miles.

On the Friday before Labor Day I walked along a stretch of it and had plenty of company. From the Kittatinny Point Visitor Center it is a comfortable four-mile walk to Sunfish Pond, the southernmost glacial lake on the A.T. It has been designated a national natural landmark by the U.S. Department of the Interior for "illustrating the natural history of the United States." Setting out, I was struck again by how quickly a hiker can leave the world of automobiles and superhighways behind. Just a few yards into the woods, I crossed a small wooden bridge over Dunnfield Creek, and the sound of the moving water was sufficient to cover the noise of Interstate 80. It was like walking through a door and closing it behind you.

Big gray squirrels with fat, luxuriant tails leapt through the trees, which were full of scolding jays. A group of Scouts came by me, then an elderly man and his granddaughter, moving fast. A family of four passed while I was having a rest. Their little girl stopped and sat beside me, puffing.

"Getting tired?" I asked.

She nodded.

"Rocky trail, isn't it?"

She nodded again, then heaved herself to her feet, and went on.

At the pond I sat on rocks at water's edge and soaked up the sun. Grouse clucked in the brush behind me as I ate my lunch. Across the pond other people sunbathed and chatted, their voices carrying across the still water. Overhead, white sailplanes from a nearby airport drifted upward on invisible thermals, like silent, soaring birds.

Across the line, in New York, I did another day hike, from Fitzgerald Falls to the Mombasha High Point and back. "On a clear day," the guidebook says, "New York City may be seen on the horizon due magnetic S." At the high point I persuaded myself I could see the World Trade Center, then double-checked my map and realized I was peering due magnetic N. Still, it was a nice walk. Light sprinkles came and went. I could hear their faint patter high in the trees, but little rain reached the ground. A few yellow leaves lay plastered on the damp trail, and a few more drifted down through the forest. Crumbling stone walls, the remnants of an abandoned settlement, meandered over ridges and hilltops. I'm always surprised to come upon something so obviously man-made deep in the woods.

On another drizzly day I came down out of the woods into Bear Mountain State Park. Roughly an hour's drive from New York City, it is a popular destination for city-weary New Yorkers. Pedal boaters bobbed on Hessian Lake. At picnic tables families ignored the drizzle to grill their lunches, making heavenly smells. Beyond the picnickers, the trail turns right, goes through a tunnel under a highway, past the swimming pool, and into the quietness of the Trailside Museum and Zoo. A justly renowned statue of Walt Whitman greeted me there. He's striding along, his hat in his hand, looking as if a little rain never bothered *him*.

I came out of the zoo onto the highway near the tollgate of Bear Mountain Bridge. On the other side, the trail over Anthony's Nose was closed temporarily during World War II after the bridge manager wrote to the ATC, "equipment carried by hikers . . . can readily be used to conceal and place high explosives. . . ."

With nothing more lethal than a Swiss army knife, I crossed over the bridge. On the other side of the Hudson, I knew, awaited one of the glories of the planet: autumn in New England. ☐

WINTERBERRY *(Gaultheria procumbens)*

ANIMALS ANIMALS/JOE MCDONALD (BELOW); ANIMALS ANIMALS/C. W. SCHWARTZ (ABOVE)

In autumn thousands of birds of prey, including
red-tailed hawks like this one, migrate along Kittatinny Ridge
in eastern Pennsylvania. People from all over the
world gather at Hawk Mountain Sanctuary,
adjacent to the A.T., to witness the spectacle. Preyed
upon by raptors, the eastern cottontail (left) has
a niche in Appalachian ecology.

FOLLOWING PAGES: Rare sight for Appalachian Trail
hikers, a red fox kit surveys its world.
ANIMALS ANIMALS/ZIG LESZCZYNSKI

Walking Softly
Above the Clouds

"Come for lunch," said Father Bosco, when I called. So I made my way to Graymoor, the Mount of Atonement Monastery about seven miles up the trail from its crossing of the Hudson River. A plump and cheerful sister directed me to the top of the mountain and the complex of buildings that make up the monastery and the retreat. From the A.T. a blue-blazed side trail leads hikers a short distance to the monastery, which, in a centuries-old tradition of Franciscan hospitality, offers them food and lodging for a night. Father Bosco Schmidt is the friar whose responsibility they become during their brief stay.

Graymoor is a splendid mountaintop, crowded with gardens and pathways that surround the old brick buildings of the monastery. As the first dead leaves of autumn came drifting down, I located Father Bosco, who escorted me to the dining room for lunch—bean soup, macaroni and cheese, rolls, custard pie, coffee. A group of guests from New York City, visiting here on retreat, stood and sang a song of friendship as we ate. Most of the friars were in civilian clothing, though a couple swept in in long brown robes; and most were elderly, a fact that worries Father Bosco. "We're not getting the young men coming to replace us," he said. He himself has lived here for 47 years.

After lunch Father Bosco showed me the accommodations available to long-distance hikers—clean, well-lighted, comfortable rooms, simply furnished. Unmarried couples are given separate rooms. "I tell 'em, 'I don't care what you do in the woods, but here you follow *our* rules,'" he said. He hands hikers a thin brochure listing rules and amenities. Showers are available to them, the dining room welcomes them, a lounge with newspapers and magazines is open to them. But "substance abuse" is strictly forbidden, and the dress code, though liberal on the subject of shorts, is fierce on footwear:

Crossing a wooded swale in New Hampshire,
Ron Fisher follows a puncheon, or hewn-log bridge, that
keeps his feet dry while protecting fragile bogland.
Blue blazes indicate side trails such as this
trek known as the Lonesome Lake Trail. White
rectangular blazes mark the A.T. from Maine to Georgia.

113

No Bare Feet at Any Time on the Property. Hikers are not charged for food or lodging, but contributions are gratefully accepted. Dozens of hikers stop by each year. "I think only a few come looking for spiritual sustenance," said Father Bosco, rather sadly. "Most are simply curious, or have heard about the free meals and beds. But they're welcome, whatever their motives."

From the sacred to the profane is a 30-mile hike through the Hudson Highlands, for after leaving Graymoor the A.T. passes near the so-called Nuclear Lake, a 50-acre body of water with a mysterious past and an unforeseeable future.

A nuclear fuels processing and research facility operated here from 1958 to 1972, when a chemical explosion forced the facility to shut down. Only after receiving official safety clearances did the Park Service acquire the property in 1979 for a relocation of the A.T. But some hikers and local citizens still worried that the area might not be safe. As a result, extensive and sophisticated tests were conducted, which detected elevated radiation levels in portions of two of the remaining buildings. The Park Service plans to carefully dismantle the old buildings and to take all necessary precautions in cleaning the site thoroughly.

No increased levels of radiation have been found on the trail itself, and the ATC and the New York–New Jersey Trail Conference believe the present route is safe. Nonetheless, all the buildings and the areas within 600 feet of the lake remain closed and posted against public entry until the cleanup is complete. Leaflets available on the trail near the lake tell the story of the mishap and offer an alternate route around the site.

Hikers often expect to find in New York dense urban areas abutting the trail and are surprised, as I was, at the sense of remoteness the state offers. Too, New York trail people have acquired extensive corridor lands, preserving many really beautiful areas along the trail's route.

By Connecticut the nature of the Appalachian countryside has changed considerably from that of the South. No crickets or worms for sale here in roadside general stores. Now well-scrubbed exurbanites tend immaculate gardens, and the cute corner garage is called Honest Engine. The A.T. runs north through the western ends of Connecticut and Massachusetts before reaching Vermont. This is the land of the lovely Housatonic River and the benign Berkshire Hills, of somber dairy cattle in lush pastures and orchards surrounded by old stone walls.

It is undemanding country for backpacking, and a hiker is never more than a few hours' walk from a town or a road. In Connecticut the trail descends Schaghticoke Mountain, traverses the ridge of Mount Algo, runs through the Housatonic State Forest, and finally climbs Bear Mountain. Entering Massachusetts near Sages Ravine, the A.T. runs a short distance along the Taconic Range before crossing a valley to the Berkshires and going on to the bucolic Tyringham Valley and Upper Goose Pond. It exits Massachusetts into Vermont north of Mount Greylock.

The Connecticut–Massachusetts trail is gentle and good-natured; the

WHITE ASH *(Fraxinus americana)*

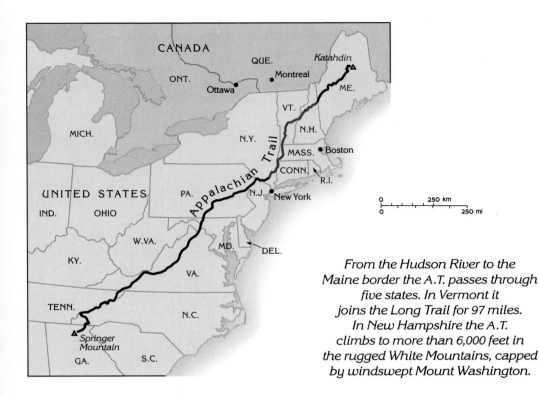

From the Hudson River to the Maine border the A.T. passes through five states. In Vermont it joins the Long Trail for 97 miles. In New Hampshire the A.T. climbs to more than 6,000 feet in the rugged White Mountains, capped by windswept Mount Washington.

countryside it passes through, quaint and settled. My first experience was typical of it, I think, as I walked south along the trail from near Cornwall Bridge one day by the hushed and shaded banks of the Housatonic to one of its tributaries—the Ten Mile River. There, just a few yards from the confluence, a 120-foot-long bridge hoists the A.T. across the Ten Mile. I stood on the bridge and admired the view. Below me, rapids gurgled toward the Housatonic, and above, a gnatcatcher sat on the uppermost twig of the uppermost branch of the uppermost limb of a dead tree, peering downstream. It flipped its tail from side to side and made occasional sallies after insects.

The bridge became a necessity a few years ago when the Park Service acquired land on both banks of the Ten Mile. It was hoped and expected that the state of Connecticut would build a bridge across the river, but public funds ran short. The Naromi Land Trust, a local conservation organization, and the Appalachian Mountain Club (AMC) came up with the $50,000 needed to build the bridge. After the footings were constructed, workers with a bulldozer, a 140-ton crane, and several flatbed trucks descended on the muddy banks of the Ten Mile and set the bridge in place over the course of two days in 1983. It's a narrow walkway, a graceful rust-colored structure, part wood, part metal. As I stood in mid-span, a kingfisher flew over my head, heading upstream fast.

There are few rivers lovelier for strolling along than the Housatonic, but property on its banks does not come cheap. In 1985 the Park Service paid

3.1 million dollars for 1,274 acres of land in the towns of Kent, Cornwall, and Sharon, in northwestern Connecticut, and for an easement on an additional 503 acres. Since early in the century, the land had been the property of the Stanley Works. The Park Service had tried, first, simply to buy a thousand-foot-wide corridor on the river's western bank, but the company wanted to retain the right to build a dam at a later date. A stalemate developed. A few years later, a consortium of Park Service people, state and local officials, trail personnel, and local business leaders worked out the details to everyone's satisfaction. The acquisition ensures permanent protection of five beautiful miles of A.T. as well as seven miles of both banks of the Housatonic, the largest and most significant river-protection measure in the state.

There were more rocks in the river than water the day I walked through. The riverbed was a bed of boulders, even though, a fisherman told me, the river was unusually high; a dam upstream regulates the flow, he said. The trail was just as I prefer it: flat and soft underfoot and shaded. A great blue heron went flapping off downstream, and a little later, in a broader and deeper stretch of the river, a party of half a dozen canoes, filled to overflowing with boisterous Boy Scouts, went paddling past.

On another day, lost among Connecticut's winding country roads, I stopped my car at a store and asked directions of the proprietor. "Where's the Appalachian Trail?" I asked. She waved an indifferent hand. "It's over there across the river someplace," she said. "There's talk of moving it, though I don't know where they'd put it; nobody wants it." While it's not quite accurate to say "nobody" wants it, certainly her attitude is not unique in this part of New England. A Connecticut landowner recently called the A.T. a multimillion-dollar "playground . . . for white, college-educated males in $80 hiking boots."

Hard feelings are found not only in Connecticut. A few miles north, in Massachusetts, the trail crosses the narrow but exquisite Tyringham Valley. Roadside driveways, fences, and stone walls here fairly bristle with No Trespassing, Private Property, Beware of Dog, and Private Drive signs. Hikers know better than to stop to ask for water.

A number of landowners have been strongly opposed to the trail here for several reasons. They are concerned about the loss of valuable land for farming or future development, and they envision a loss of privacy from the trail. They also fear litter and the installation of parking lots and picnic tables for hikers, and even forest fires that might be accidentally started by careless campers. In addition, town officials regret the loss of tax revenues when land passes into federal ownership. But Chuck Rinaldi, manager of the Park Service's Appalachian Trail Project Office, in Harpers Ferry, points out that such fears usually turn out to be groundless.

As of July 1988 the Park Service had acquired 1,712 parcels of land encompassing 517 miles of trail and 78,254 acres; and the Forest Service had acquired thousands of acres in several hundred tracts that protect 842 miles of trail. Nearly all of this land was obtained through easements or

AMERICAN BASSWOOD *(Tilia americana)*

purchases at market value as established by independent appraisals. Only 2,374 acres, affecting 58 landowners, were acquired by eminent domain.

It helps to recall that land acquisition for the A.T.—as for many of our public lands—may inconvenience a few but in the long run benefit many. "The A.T. is not an elitist resource," Dave Sherman told me. "Hikers are all ages and both sexes. They are students, farmers, dentists, truck drivers, teachers, the unemployed, chemists. They are grandmothers and teenagers, rich and poor, black and white. They are a cross section of Americans."

Just before passing out of Massachusetts into Vermont, the trail reaches the highest point in the state, crossing the 3,491-foot summit of Mount Greylock. The mountain sits in the midst of the Mount Greylock State Reservation, more than 11,000 acres of dramatic wooded hills in the northwest corner of the state, with 35 miles of hiking trails running through them. At the top is Bascom Lodge, a stone-and-wood building built by the CCC in the 1930s and now leased from the state by the AMC. Inside, stone fireplaces, high ceilings, and hand-cut oak beams lend a warm charm. Hikers can take advantage of the lodging and family-style meals it offers, but some head straight for the snack bar.

The wind was howling the day I reached the top, and the fog was so thick visibility barely existed. Walking toward the summit through a thick cloud, the hood of my parka tightly laced around my face, I was a little spooked by a huge, gray shape looming up out of the gloom—a tower honoring the men and women of Massachusetts who have sacrificed their lives in war. Nearby, in the wind and the fog, ham radio hobbyists were climbing antennas and towers, installing equipment for a weekend competition. The wind made their towers sway, and they scrambled wraith-like through the swirling fog and cold, as hunched and bundled as children let out to play.

Inside, a woman hiker was taking advantage of the shelter offered by the lodge to reorganize her pack. We talked for a bit about backpacking as she cleaned the fuel line of her tiny camp stove. "I have some time, and I have some money," she told me. "I'll hike till one or the other runs out."

A famous range of mountains awaits hikers just across the state line in Vermont. The Green Mountains reach from Massachusetts to Canada, the full length of Vermont. Most of the peaks are below 4,000 feet, and the ridgeline averages about 2,000 feet. Sugar maple and beech clothe the lower reaches, yellow and white birch and red spruce appear higher up, and above 3,000 feet red spruce and balsam fir flourish. As the elevation increases, balsam fir predominates.

It was here in the Green Mountains that I finally resolved a question that had been worrying me for months: Why does it seem as if the trail is mostly uphill? Because you hike downhill three times as fast as you hike uphill, so you spend three times as much *time* climbing. Therefore . . .

It was here, too, that photographer Sam Abell asked a memorable question. Walking through the forest one day, he idly wondered: "How long does it take to hike two and a half hours?" "About five miles," I said.

The forests of New England have taken a pounding from both man and nature over the centuries. In 1600, historians say, forests covered 96 percent of the land of New England. In the 1620s European settlement and subsistence farming began. The first sawmill opened 10 years later, and by 1700 the first regulations against overcutting were in effect near Boston.

At the time of the American Revolution forests covered 91 percent of the land, but by 1800 the international market for lumber had grown. The first pulp mill opened in the 1870s, and there was extensive cutting of timber for charcoal manufacture. Annual firewood use peaked at 4.1 million cords in 1880 but declined as the use of oil and gas as heating fuels increased. Forests now covered just 58 percent of New England.

By the early 1900s the region was no longer self-sufficient in lumber. Annual timber harvest far exceeded growth. The chestnut blight and the Dutch elm disease, among other introduced diseases, were killing trees. In addition, the gypsy moth was causing major damage by defoliation.

In the forties the blight had virtually eliminated chestnut trees, but the forest had increased once again to cover 74 percent of the land. In the fifties annual pulpwood harvest exceeded both firewood and lumber harvests, and it was estimated that 40 percent of the forest was less than 20 years old.

The oil embargo in 1973 helped increase the annual use of firewood to half a million cords in the seventies, and by the eighties annual use reached three and a half million cords, near its historic high. But forest now covers 80 percent of the land of New England, and growth is twice the annual harvest.

A serious threat to the forests in the future will likely be air pollutants. Between 1965 and 1979, for example, researchers found a 50 percent reduction in the density of spruce trees on Camels Hump, in Vermont, and most are convinced that air pollution is at least partly responsible. The haze that hangs over the mountains, scientists have found, is not solely humidity, but rather a complex brew of moisture and various air pollutants. Also, researchers have found that cloud water is considerably contaminated with heavy metals and acidic pollutants, so the lovely fingers of mist and clouds that float through the high forest all across New England give little respite to trees already struggling to survive in the harsh mountain environment.

The Green Mountains have been important to recreation since shortly before the Civil War, when tourist "summit houses" began appearing on some of them. But the Green Mountains' most famous recreational feature is the Long Trail, a 265-mile-long footpath completed in 1930 that runs along their spine from Massachusetts to Canada. Feisty Vermonters, in their *Guide Book of the Long Trail,* brag that their trail is "for the most part 'unimproved.' By design, no effort has been made to provide artificial surfacing, switchbacks, and other amenities found on highly engineered trails." The Long Trail, they say, is "steep, boggy, and rugged." The A.T. coincides with the Long Trail in Vermont from the Massachusetts line to Sherburne Pass, a distance of 97 miles, mostly in the Green Mountain National Forest.

I met a young backpacker on the trail, a high school boy with a message stitched across the front of his cap: "I Am Really Mad." It was the favorite saying, he told me, of his basketball coach.

The Long Trail, conceived on Stratton Mountain by James Taylor in 1909, and begun in 1910, predates the A.T. by several years, thus ranking as one of the oldest long-distance hiking trails in the U.S. In fact, Benton MacKaye once said that it may have been while atop Stratton Mountain —

from where he could see the long chain of the Appalachians running north and south—that he first envisioned a footpath running their length. So Stratton Mountain is something of a shrine to backpackers. A fire tower on the summit today gives them essentially the same view MacKaye had. The A.T., which now skirts the mountain, will soon run over the summit as it once did. (Editor's note: This relocation was completed in 1988.) The Nature Conservancy purchased Stratton Pond and most of the mountain for 3.2 million dollars from a paper company in 1986 and conveyed it to the Forest Service for inclusion in the Green Mountain National Forest.

A few miles up the trail is a sadder shrine, a bridge built across Clarendon Gorge in memory of a young man who drowned here some years ago while crossing the flooded Mill River after the bridge had been washed away. The night before I walked through the gorge, there had been flood warnings for southern Vermont, so I was glad the present bridge existed. It would have been suicidal to try to ford the river. Chocolate-colored water in fearful spate thundered beneath my feet.

It is a suspension bridge, its narrow floor made up of two-by-sixes running lengthwise, with cables waist high to hang on to. At each step the bridge bobs up and down and gives the bottom of your foot a little slap. At the head of the bridge is a plaque memorializing the drowned backpacker: "Bob Brugmann, Feb. 18, 1956—July 4, 1973. Lost at this site while hiking the trail he loved. . . ."

The mountains of Vermont witnessed a revolution of sorts back in the thirties. Snowshoeing had been a popular pastime, with overnight excursions to distant camps through the deep and silent snow a favored activity. But when the Norwegians and Austrians arrived with their skis and skiing techniques, snowshoeing quickly lost out to the more exciting and faster sport. America's first ski lift—an "endless rope tow" powered by a Model T engine—was invented here in Vermont not far from the A.T. Since then, ski areas have sprawled atop many of the same peaks the hiking trails use, scarring the mountaintops with ski trails and noisy aerial ski lifts, while the valleys have filled with condominiums and parking lots. As a result, hikers and skiers have sometimes annoyed one another like ranchers and farmers. Vermont attempted to crack down in the sixties with legislation controlling development above 2,500 feet, but ski developments have continued to grow, and the A.T. and the ski trails still sometimes run afoul of one another.

Just half a mile north of Sherburne Pass, the A.T. and the Long Trail diverge, the Long Trail continuing north to Canada and the A.T. swinging east toward the Connecticut River and New Hampshire. Here the trail crosses many ridges between two distinct mountain ranges, the Greens of Vermont and the Whites of New Hampshire. Much of it follows old logging roads, rough and overgrown. Farther on, it runs through a patchwork of wooded and cleared hills—evidence of the extensive farming that once took place in this part of Vermont. Finally, the trail crosses many low, forested hills as it approaches the Connecticut River. *(Continued on page 130)*

EASTERN HEMLOCK *(Tsuga canadensis)*

*"I'm an outdoor guy who
loves evergreens," says Father Bosco
Schmidt of Graymoor,
a monastery overlooking
the Hudson River Valley. "Since 1959
I've planted more than 2,000
white pine, Norway spruce, and
Colorado blue spruce."
He recalls that in 1970 a hiker
stumbled in and a tradition began—
free meals and lodging for one night.
Joe-pye weed and goldenrod
(below) edge the A.T.
along the Housatonic River
in Connecticut.*

*Gossamer wheel of an orb spider
shimmers in a dew-spangled forest in
Massachusetts. From spinnerets—
such as those on the lower
abdomen of the black and yellow
garden spider above—orb weavers reel
out silk threads to fashion
nature's most spectacular webs. The
nearly invisible masterpieces of
engineering net meals for their builders.*

*Dairy farmers and maple sugar producers four generations strong, the
Hales of Sunset Farm gather on the porch of the original house
on their 400-acre homestead in Tyringham, Massachusetts. The A.T.*

crosses soil the Hales once tilled. "In 1985 we sold 48 acres to the government," family patriarch Arnold Hale says, "so the Appalachian Trail could be moved off main roads into fields and woods."

Tap and tube replace tap and bucket for
collecting sugary maple sap. Fred and Claude Kimberley
(opposite) drill a tap hole in one of 8,000 sugar
trees on the Hale farm. Wafting around Arnold Hale and
great-grandson R. C. Bienvenue, steam
from boiling sap turns the sugarhouse misty (below).
Young R. C. sneaks a taste while checking a hydrometer
reading. It takes a temperature of 219°F to drive off water, kill
bacteria, and leave pure syrup ready for marketing.

FOLLOWING PAGES: From atop Mount Greylock, at 3,491
feet the highest point in Massachusetts, the A.T. overlooks
ridges rolling toward Vermont's Green Mountains.

CHRIS JOHNS (ALL)

(Continued from page 119) It crosses the Connecticut River and continues into downtown Hanover on West Wheelock Street. A sign along-side the sidewalk brought home to me how near the end of the trail I was: 437 miles to Katahdin. Almost 80 percent of the A.T. was now behind me.

Hanover is home to Dartmouth College, and its handsome Georgian buildings ring the Dartmouth College green. The A.T. encounters a traffic light and touches a corner of the campus before turning and heading down Main Street, so I sat on a bench for a bit and watched the students' spare-time activities on the green. A couple of touch football games were in progress, and Frisbees sailed through the air. A group chose up sides for a game of lacrosse: They dropped all their sticks—called "crosses"—into a pile, then one player randomly tossed them aside, left, right, left, right. Presto, the teams were chosen.

The trail here makes another of those outlandish tours through a down-town: past the Hanover Inn and a movie theater, past restaurants and banks, past florists and drugstores. I browsed for a bit in the Dartmouth Book Store and did something I seldom do, bought a book purely because I liked its title—*On Sledge and Horseback to Outcast Siberian Lepers,* by Kate Marsden. First published in 1892, it's been around awhile. Pretty good book, too, as it turned out.

Another huge forest—the 763,000-acre White Mountain National Forest—sprawls across much of northern New Hampshire and into western Maine. The A.T. wends its way through the White Mountains and the Presidentials, a famous subrange, reaching its highest point north of the Smokies. Nearly 13 miles of the trail in the Presidential Range lie above tree line, and since air temperature tends to decrease three to six degrees for every thousand feet of elevation, the trail here, sometimes well above 5,000 feet, is often a cold and windy place.

The Appalachian Mountain Club maintains a string of eight huts along the A.T. over a distance of 56 miles in the White Mountains. They offer over-night lodging and meals during the summer and are operated by young men and women. At one hut I ran across a thru-hiker—Larry Jackson—who had just finished. He had started the previous March, without the benefit of a guidebook. "I knew the trail began somewhere in northern Georgia," he told me, "and I thought if I could just get to Gainesville, I'd be close." He took a bus to Gainesville and asked around. "No one had *heard* of the Appalachian Trail!" He arranged with a taxi driver to take him to the trailhead nearest Springer Mountain. "Cost me $40, but at least I was on my way." He was on the trail during the year's late spring snows. "It was *cold!* I did push-ups in my sleeping bag, trying to get warm."

Most thru-hikers, operating on a tight budget, find the huts too expensive to use and camp instead in the backcountry at designated tent sites and shelters, or they erect their tents elsewhere in the forest, out of sight of the trail. Some of the shelters have live-in seasonal caretakers who collect a small fee to help defray costs, as well as maintain trail. So backpackers here can choose from a spectrum of accommodations that range from primitive off-trail camping to the relative luxury of staying in the huts.

Sam and I one day rode a tramway to the top of Cannon Mountain, then walked a couple of miles to the Lonesome Lake Hut, back on the A.T., to spend the night. Scrambled a couple of miles, really, for much of the way was *steeply* downhill, through scrubby brush and across mossy boulders. The hut, sheltered by paper birches and balsam firs, sits near the lake. It has a main building and two bunkhouses that will hold 44 people overnight. When we arrived, ducks were standing on their heads in the middle of the shallow lake, feeding in the twilight.

It was late in the season, and except for the two caretakers, we had for company only Rich White, a thru-hiker, and his father, who was joining him for a few days. Rich was several weeks behind the body of the year's long-distance hikers, and while we were all together in the hut's spacious kitchen preparing our evening meal and coffee, he explained why: "I ran out of money," he laughed. He figured it cost about a dollar a mile to hike the A.T.—"not counting what you have to spend to equip yourself in the first place."

So he took a break from hiking. "I stopped when I got to the Delaware Water Gap and went home to Massachusetts and worked in the dining room of an inn for three weeks to earn money. I'd tell customers I was working to make enough to finish the A.T., and they'd leave me bigger tips." His trail name—the Berkshire Bear—honored the athletes of his high school teams.

I was struck again by the efficiency of the thru-hikers' grapevine. Rich knew the whereabouts and welfare of practically all of his compatriots. So-and-so had dropped out and gone home to Canada; somebody else had sprained an ankle and was recuperating in Monson. He knew about people who were a week ahead of him and others who were two days behind.

The grapevine had warned him of the Three Devil Dogs near Killington that come out to bark at backpackers. He told us about the two backpackers—We Two Boys—whose reputation as gourmet trail cooks we'd already heard of. "They're even packing a *whisk!*" he said. He knew trail gossip and told us a racy story about a woman hiker and a guide she had hired to help her get to Maine.

It was chilly in the morning when we left the hut for our walk down to the highway. Hewn-log bridges crossed boggy spots, and in places the trail was practically solid tree roots, evidence of the millions of footsteps that have fallen on these old trails in the White Mountains. The clouds were scudding by fast overhead, the aspens were yellow and the maples red, and leaves came drifting down around us like snow as we walked.

It was easy to find dramatic contrasts on the trail in the Whites. We stood in the darkness one evening on the bank of the Ellis River in Pinkham Notch as beavers worked into the night. Flashlights didn't bother them; perhaps they appreciated the help. But the slightest noise made them dive. It was serene and warm and quiet.

Atop 6,288-foot Mount Washington, on the other hand, the elements were raw and noisy. The highest point in New England, the mountain can be a fearsome place, with severe weather and violent winds. The wind in 1934 reached 231 miles an hour, the strongest natural land-surface wind speed

SUGAR MAPLE *(Acer saccharum)*

ever recorded in the world. P.T. Barnum called the view from here "the second greatest show on earth." Ravens circle high above the cold stones and alpine plants of the summit.

Hiking is one way to reach the top. The Mount Washington Cog Railway, opened in 1869, is another. At its steepest point, crossing Jacob's Ladder, the grade exceeds 37 percent. And a carriage road, begun in 1854 and completed in 1861, climbs eight miles from the highway to the summit. Horse-drawn mountain wagons hauled sightseers to the top, where they could dine — and even spend the night — in a series of summit hotels. Now the old carriage road is the Mount Washington Auto Road.

Near Gorham I visited with Doug Philbrook, president of the company that manages the auto road. "In the early days," said Doug, "it took about four hours, to get to the top by mountain wagon, with six horses pulling. Sometimes people would start at Crawford Notch and go up on the cog railway, then down the other side on the carriage road to Pinkham Notch. In 1911 the road was opened to private automobiles, and today 83 percent of the people who use it drive their own cars, while the remainder take advantage of the stage service."

The notches in the White Mountains are our old friends, the gaps. Crawford Notch, the most famous, had a narrow Indian path through it, which became a road in the 1770s, a tortuous route that crossed the Saco River 32 times. The first cargo through the mountains on this road, it is reported, was a keg of rum. In 1819, Abel Crawford and his son Ethan Allen Crawford cut the first path to the summit of Mount Washington, a route still followed in part by the A.T. and considered to be the oldest continuously maintained mountain trail in the country. Father and son also built hostelries in the notch. Trail builders, innkeepers, mountain guides — the Crawford family, for whom the notch was named, had a lasting impact on the area.

The Appalachian Mountain Club — founded in Boston in 1876 and the oldest of the ATC member clubs — took as one of its earliest priorities the building of trails in the White Mountains, or "paths," as they were then called. In the first 50 years of the club's existence, hundreds of miles of trail were blazed in the White Mountains — much of it by AMC volunteers. But the trails were so scattered through the mountains that maintaining them became as much of a challenge as building them. In 1919 the club began hiring students during the summer for the maintenance work. Thus was born the AMC trail crew. Paid a modest salary and given room and board, the 20 or so crew members live in the field during the week, clearing and maintaining the hundreds of miles of trail the AMC cares for in New Hampshire and Maine.

Coming down out of the Presidential Range on the Appalachian Trail is like falling out of an airplane. From the summit of Mount Madison, at 5,366 feet, it is a steep 2.4 miles to the West Branch of the Peabody River, 3,138 feet below.

It was a crisp and cool autumn day when I walked steeply down some man-made stone steps off Middle Moriah Mountain to the first narrow trickle of the Rattle River. I sat for a bit and let my sweaty shirt dry. After the austerity and fury of the high Presidentials — those bare, windblown summits with cairns marking the trail — it was good to be back in the realm of

132

woodpeckers: I could hear them working around me. From here down, the trail would gentle as it followed the river. The sun felt good on my back, but when a cloud with a gray center passed over and a breeze sprang up, I remembered that it was fall and went on my way.

It was impossible to walk quietly on the dead leaves: *crunch crunch crunch*—I rustled like a bear. But warblers ignored me and hung upside down as they foraged for bugs. Somewhere I could hear running water. Soon I came to a scene of carnage, a trailside boulder that had been used as a table by some creature: a handful of blue jay feathers, along with bits of gristle and bone, was scattered over it. I walked for a while alongside the still-narrow river, full of mini-waterfalls and tiny rapids. A downy woodpecker clung to a tree, working. Black and white, little red cap—he looked color-coordinated, as if he had spent some time selecting his outfit.

In a little while I crossed the Rattle River on some huge gray boulders. In quiet pools in midstream, long-legged water bugs darted out of my shadow. Ten minutes later, I recrossed the river, for no reason that was apparent to me. But it was an easy place to cross, and I like to imagine that the people who lay out trails sometimes give hikers something different to do just for the heck of it.

I stopped for a rest and an apple and some peanuts at the Rattle River Shelter. Someone had left a tattered paperback there, *Star Wars: From the Adventures of Luke Skywalker.* "Another galaxy, another time. . . ."

I watched another downy remove some bark from a tree, find something, and gobble it down with a quick and satisfied *gulp*. On down the gentle slope I continued, humming. "I sing because I'm happy, I sing because I'm free, For His eye is on the sparrow, And I know He watches me." The trail was full of red leaves and rocks, and small, shrubby evergreens grew alongside it. The river burbled at my side. It was 20 feet wide now, and leaves a dozen shades of yellow floated in it.

Suddenly, a spot of red flitted through the trees far ahead, and it took me a moment to realize it was a car on U.S. Route 2.

Civilization. ☐

NANNYBERRY *(Viburnum lentago)*

Sunset veil of clouds draws across
a slope in the Green Mountains. The A.T. rides
the ridge beyond a church tower
in Bennington, Vermont. Queen Anne's
lace accents showy blossoms of
wild bergamot (below).

FOLLOWING PAGES: On a rainy afternoon,
hikers on a Vermont byway
pause near a venerable sugar maple.

Viewed from the ice-choked Ammonoosuc River,
Mount Washington—flanked by Mount Clay to the left—
stands gripped in arctic cold. Dominating
New Hampshire's Presidential Range, this 6,288-foot
peak has the world's severest weather outside the polar regions.
Condensing and then evaporating moisture
created the lenticular cloud hovering over the summit.
Below, cross-country skiers Michael Russom and Karen Geriak
enjoy a shelter in winter. Summer brings
heavy use as hikers stride toward Stratton Pond,
one of Vermont's most visited A.T. sites.

FOLLOWING PAGES: Thundering Brook Falls, one of the
highest in Vermont, cascades past Dave Sherman, hiking
near Gifford Woods State Park.

© DAVID MUENCH 1988 (OPPOSITE); CHRIS JOHNS (ABOVE)

*Climbers, leapers, and swimmers dwell in the
woodlands of New Hampshire and Vermont. A marten
prefers a conifer perch. The wood frog, crouched
among fallen cherries (above), chooses a habitat of
concealing ground cover. More venturesome,
a raccoon boldly wades after crayfish.*

ANIMALS ANIMALS/LEONARD LEE RUE III (OPPOSITE); ANIMALS ANIMALS/BRECK P. KENT (ABOVE)

*Autumn in New Hampshire's
White Mountains sets sugar maples
ablaze but leaves red spruce unchanged
in Glen Ellis gorge, near the trail.
The A.T. takes travelers past shaggy
scalecap mushrooms clustered
on a decaying paper birch log (below).*

*FOLLOWING PAGES: From the summit
of Mount Liberty, in the
White Mountains, a hiker surveys
Little Haystack Mountain
and Mounts Lincoln and Garfield, where
the A.T. traverses the ridgeline.*
SYD NISBET

TOM ALGIRE (OPPOSITE)

144

Alpine hostel for hikers in New Hampshire, Greenleaf Hut provides cozy
lodging, warm fellowship, and nutritious meals, including
pita bread (below). This hut and seven others built by the Appalachian
Mountain Club form a chain of high-country havens spaced
conveniently along the A.T. across the White Mountains. Hardy and
cheerful hut crew members, such as Mariel Feider (opposite), wear many
hats at once—host, cook, custodian, and dispenser of trail lore.

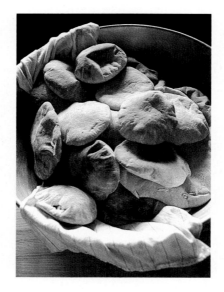

*Treadway to the clouds
leads backpackers up 5,260-foot
Mount Lafayette,
the highest climb in
New Hampshire's Franconia
Range. Above tree
line and often buffeted by harsh,
freezing winds, this stretch
offers memorable
views. The cairn serves as
a trail marker. The
trudging party carefully
keeps to the stony
path, protecting fragile
alpine tundra from an eroding
stream of footsteps.*

151

*Alongside the Appalachian Trail, reflections of
October fill Lost Pond, near Pinkham Notch, in the White
Mountains. Visitors at Pinkham Notch Camp, as
well as A.T. hikers, enjoy the tranquillity
of this shallow pond. Woodland sunflowers (below)
dab added color on a palette of trail foliage.*

FOLLOWING PAGES: *Chalky bark distinguishes a
screen of paper and gray birches in New Hampshire's
Ammonoosuc River Valley.*

© DAVID MUENCH 1988

*"Autumn in the White Mountains
is a glorious benediction,"
says 90-year-old Phyllis Kimball,
a lifelong resident of
New Hampshire. "Maple leaves
are my favorite. I arrange them
in sprays of color and decorate the
rustic cabins I rent to
people wanting to get away
from civilization."
Fall colors, a church steeple
(opposite), a pastor's posted
exclamation—all evoke spiritual
feelings often shared by
hikers close to nature on the A.T.*

FOLLOWING PAGES: In the Tyringham Valley of Massachusetts, twin sugar maples along the A.T. sweeten the passage of autumn in New England.

MIKE WARREN

Old Friends, Ancient Mountains

A far country indeed is Maine. A sign outside a roadside taxidermist's in Brownville Junction said, "Bear Parts Wanted." (As for me, I wanted no part of any bear.) Here in Maine a real wilderness stretches for miles, broken only by the occasional road. The mountains, though not high by the world's standards, climb in places to satisfyingly lofty peaks, and their primeval slopes and valleys have a character as distinctive as a Yankee twang. But it is the seemingly endless forest—the famous North Woods—that brings hikers back again and again.

As it has again brought me back.

In 1972 I wrote another book about the Appalachian Trail, also for the National Geographic Society. For both books I explored the length of the trail and the character of the land along it. And I spent time getting to know some of the people who use the Appalachian Trail and others who care for it.

Although it still runs through the same eternal mountains, this wilderness path has changed significantly since 1972. For example, more of it ran along country roads or across private property then, probably half of it. I remember long walks on blacktop highways and through farmers' gates and pastures. Protective legislation was in place in 1972, but the actual acquisition of land outside federal parks and forests had barely begun. Now Congress and the ATC and its partner clubs have succeeded in getting most of the trail up into the hills where it belongs. The major change since 1972, however, is the protected corridor, averaging a thousand feet in width, which most of the trail now runs through.

I seem to remember more chipmunks but fewer birds in the forests in 1972, forests that seemed eerily quiet to me then. Now, though some say

Trail's end, the fog-capped summit of Katahdin
rises above the lakes and forests of Maine's
storied North Woods. Fiery maple leaves tell of autumn's
arrival. Hikers here must hurry to beat the
unpredictable snows of winter. Above, a wooden
trail symbol weathers on a paper birch.

© DAVID MUENCH 1988 (OPPOSITE)

there has been a *decrease* in the actual number of songbirds in the Appalachians, there's seldom a time in spring or early summer when you can't hear them singing or see one flitting from branch to branch. The protected corridor may be concentrating them nearer the trail, and—what with all the relocations—the trail itself may now be running through more inviting and suitable bird habitat.

In 1972 backpacking was perhaps at its peak of popularity as a sport, so the trail was probably more crowded than it is today. Now it's possible to find places where you can feel alone in the woods, which is after all one of the major appeals of backpacking.

For me, air mattresses were softer in 1972. Hills were not so steep nor mornings quite so cold. Knees were not a problem. I met a hiker on this trip who remembered photographs of me in the earlier book. "But your beard was *brown* then," he said. (Not white, he might have added.)

But the forests of Maine are just as I remember them: quiet, damp, shaded, and soft. Light still dapples the ferns and mosses of the moist forest floor, and pine trees creak and moan in even a gentle breeze. Rocky streams gurgle through practically every valley.

The A.T. enters Maine through a dramatic gateway: Mahoosuc Notch, another of those gaps in the mountains. The 30-mile-long Mahoosuc Range is one of the finest stretches of mountains on the A.T. Some hikers compare it with the rugged Cheoahs in the South, between the Nantahala Range and the Smokies. Mahoosuc Notch is barely a mile long and only a few yards wide. Over millennia boulders have tumbled down into the notch, creating a jumbled obstacle course for the trail to find its way through. It's so shaded that ice in some of the deep crevices lasts until July. You scramble over, under, and around boulders as big as trucks, with the notch walls rising higher and higher on either side. In some places, backpackers must take off their packs and drag them along as they squeeze under boulders or through caves. This stretch of trail is sometimes called the toughest mile on the A.T., and tough it is—but fun too, if you're not in a hurry.

S am and I arrived at the notch just as a backpacker was emerging from it. He had been on the trail several days and was suffering: He had underestimated his rate of sugar consumption and had already exhausted his candy supply. Desperate for sweets, he cleaned me out of M&Ms and went gratefully on his way.

As Sam and I clambered through the notch, we came upon a dead moose among the boulders. It had evidently fallen from the cliffs above, perhaps slipping on snow or ice earlier in the year. It appeared to be a calf and was sprawled awkwardly, like a broken and discarded toy.

Maine seemed like a state of endings to me. Though the Appalachians continue northward to the Gaspé Peninsula, the trail ends here. Though hundreds of people worked for years building the trail, they finished here. Though friendships formed on the trail by thru-hikers may last for years, there is a parting of the ways in Maine. And though ceremonies marking the

AMERICAN BEECH *(Fagus grandifolia)*

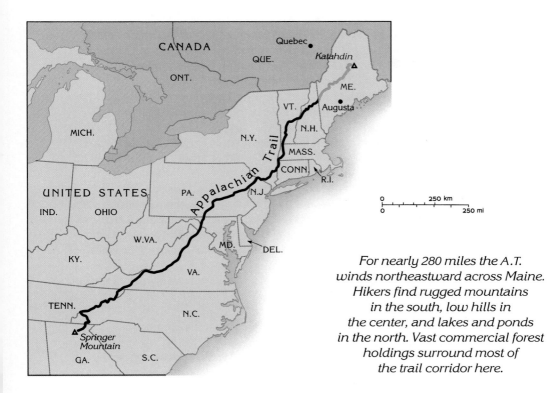

For nearly 280 miles the A.T. winds northeastward across Maine. Hikers find rugged mountains in the south, low hills in the center, and lakes and ponds in the north. Vast commercial forest holdings surround most of the trail corridor here.

completion of the trail had taken place up and down its length all year, one of the last was held on August 14, the golden anniversary of the completion, near Carrabassett.

It was a particularly touching ceremony, as it honored not only the trail but also the CCC veterans who had completed it. One in particular, Myles Fenton, who lives now in Sorrento, had worked on the very last section of the trail—on the very day of completion.

After a final go-round of the year's speeches ("little trees grow up to be big trees...," Ray Hunt reminded us) at the Carrabassett Valley Ski Tour Center, we rode a gondola to the summit of Sugarloaf Mountain and hiked two miles to a place on the A.T. where a commemorative plaque was to be mounted. Myles, who was 69 at the time, and his wife of 46 years, Evon, made the walk with the rest of us, down the rocky trail and through the tangled shrubs and trees of Sugarloaf and along a saddle to a huge boulder whose surface had been prepared to accept a plaque. Sören Siren, a young member of the Maine Conservation Corps, itself a sort of descendant of the CCC, carried the heavy bronze plaque. At the boulder he and Myles posed with it in place, as a couple of dozen photographers and journalists jostled for position and struggled to get Sören's name right.

Someone asked Myles if he remembered the boulder. "Remember it! I remember moving it off the trail," he joked.

There was an overlook he *did* remember, though, at the end of a short side trail he had helped clear. At the rocky outcrop the vista was of forested valleys and mountains that turned blue as they receded into the distance.

I happened to ride back down the mountain in the gondola with Myles and Evon. "Did you enjoy your day?" I asked Myles.

"Im-*mense*-ly," he said. "Though I'm a little embarrassed by all the attention. There were a lot of others besides me who worked on the trail. I'm sorry they can't be with us here today."

"I think it's only fairly recently," added Evon, "that most people are beginning to appreciate the *quality* of work and the *amount* of work that the CCC boys did. It's really very impressive."

As we bobbed and swayed slowly down the mountain, dangling from a cable in a small, six-passenger car, I did some calculating and determined that Myles and Evon must have met around the time the trail was being finished. "You're right," said Myles. "We met at the Methodist Church in Bridgton. Some of the CCC boys would go over there to church, just to meet girls. They seemed to congregate there."

Evon looked at him with some surprise. "Well, why do you suppose that was?" she said. "That's where all you *boys* were."

The trail that Myles helped complete runs northeastward for nearly 280 tough miles from the New Hampshire line to Baxter Peak, the summit of Katahdin. And the rivers and streams that flow from the mountains of Maine can give a backpacker pause. Fewer bridges span these streams than in more settled areas, and in a number of places hikers are likely to get their feet wet. By far the biggest stream they must ford is the Kennebec River, where the trail crosses to the village of Caratunk. This is the "most formidable water ford" along the entire A.T., the trail guide warns. "The river is approximately a hundred yards wide with a swift, powerful current. Its depth varies greatly as the river is used for hydroelectric power generation." Fording has never been a satisfactory arrangement and is in fact dangerous. In 1985 a Georgia woman lost her footing while fording the river here, was dragged down by her heavy pack, and drowned.

So in 1987 the Maine Appalachian Trail Club and the ATC contracted with Rolling Thunder, a white-water rafting outfitter, to ferry hikers across the Kennebec. Lanky Chuck Dunn, of Rolling Thunder, took me for a canoe ride to the spot where the trail crosses the river.

"The Kennebec is a bold river, one of the last monuments before reaching Katahdin," he said. "It takes maybe 15 minutes to ford it, but thru-hikers look forward to it for weeks. They still can ford the river if they want to," he continued. "But we're here with a canoe nearly every day between May and October from 10 a.m. to noon. In 1987 we ferried some 265 people across."

Up the trail from the Kennebec is Monson, another of those little trail towns that backpackers are grateful to reach, and along whose streets they wander—from the post office to the general store to the do-it-yourself laundry. On one of the front lawns of Pleasant Street, the route of the A.T. through town, stands a wooden, bearded backpacker, a colorfully painted

EASTERN WHITE PINE *(Pinus strobus)*

signboard. Shaw's Boarding Home, long a favored stop of Maine hikers, offers hot showers, comfortable beds, a washer and dryer, and all you can eat to footsore backpackers. Keith and Pat Shaw preside.

I've stayed at Shaw's a number of times on various trips through town and always enjoy the conversations with fellow backpackers, always overeat, always depart regretfully. It was at Shaw's that I met two backpackers who were planning a visit to a "broken hiker," Pokey Balboa, who had fractured a leg. Pokey was famed for turning up interesting junk while "poking around." He had once found a 30-pound bear trap near the trail and had toted it to the next post office.

A born tinkerer, Keith Shaw always seems to be in the midst of making another renovation or contemplating another addition to his already complicated house. For business is booming. "We had about 600 stay here last year," Keith told me. "Not all hikers. We get hunters and skiers and fishermen, too." Pat is prepared to feed anyone who shows up, but wishes there was a way they could let her know they're coming. "People come wandering in off the trail at all hours, wanting a home-cooked meal," she said. "I'm glad to oblige, but it's hard to plan, not knowing how many there'll be."

A proposed relocation will divert the trail around Monson, but a side trail will continue to lead hikers toward Shaw's.

North of Monson stretches the "100-mile wilderness," so called because it is the longest section of the A.T. anywhere that touches neither highways nor towns. The trail crosses a couple of small but rugged mountain ranges—the Barren-Chairback Range and the White Cap Range—then wanders among lakes and boggy ponds before reaching Abol Bridge Campground, just south of Baxter State Park. In all that distance it crosses just ten gravel logging roads deep within holdings of several large paper companies.

The pine, fir, and spruce forests of Maine—nearly 17 million acres—cover about 90 percent of the land area of the state. They have been cut four times since the early 1700s, and are now logged primarily for Maine's forest products mills. Our image of the Maine woodsman—a rough-and-tumble lumberjack in a plaid shirt with an ax and an ox—was formed before the Civil War, when the forests were logged, and felled trees were dragged to streams and floated to lumber mills on the rivers. A billion board feet of lumber was the average yearly cut of the state during the Civil War period.

A change that affected the A.T. came in 1974, when loggers were prohibited from using the rivers in Maine to float their logs to the mills. Now, trucks and railcars must carry the timber. Overland hauling has meant the construction of gravel roads in the forests, roads that often touch the trail corridor and in some places cross it.

I set off from north of Monson one day in May, hoping—as I had a year earlier in Georgia—for signs of spring and hoping, too, to get to Abol Bridge. Instead, I got a lesson in the things that can go wrong with a hike.

It started off well enough, with sunshine and cool breezes. But later the crossing of Long Pond Stream was tricky. The water was high and fast, tumbling over slippery boulders. It was my first hike of the year, and my pack felt top-heavy and awkward. I inched across, watched by a local youth who, I think, was secretly hoping I'd fall in.

My first destination was Cloud Pond Lean-to, some five miles from where I started. It meant a climb of Barren Mountain, a long and arduous haul to its 2,660-foot summit that soon had me puffing. Another hymn: "I'm pressing on the upward way, New heights I'm gaining ev'ry day; Still praying as I onward bound, 'Lord, plant my feet on higher ground.' " At the Barren Ledges, an overlook about two-thirds of the way to the top, I stopped for a rest and a drink of water. Below me a white airplane, with pontoons instead of wheels, buzzed past on its way up the valley.

Later I witnessed a small drama. I came upon a red squirrel sitting in the crotch of a tree, chattering angrily. At first I thought I had disturbed it, but as I got closer it became apparent something else was bothering it. It was hovering near a huge clump of roots and vegetation where a tree had fallen. Unexpectedly, from a hole in this big mass, a face appeared, a fuzzy, weasel-like face—a marten. Both surprised, we regarded each other for a moment, then the marten went loping off through the forest. The squirrel followed along, up in the trees, still jabbering. In a minute it was back. It went to the hole where the marten had emerged and dangled from its hind legs above it. It was very quiet now and quivering with fright. It sniffed deeply, then went back to the fork of the tree, where it sat, shivering.

At the summit of Barren Mountain I leaned against an abandoned fire tower and had some lunch, as the first bumblebee of spring, looking small and pale, flew in circles and bumped into things.

The lean-to stood on the edge of Cloud Pond, a name that might have referred to the swarms of mosquitoes and blackflies that rose from its marshy shores. I had been warned that Maine was having an especially severe crop of insects this year and had noticed them as I hiked. Every time I stopped for a minute, a cloud would form around my head, and I'd feel them settling lightly on my legs and arms. They're not biting, I told myself. But I was unprepared for the hosts that settled upon me at the pond. I had four kinds of repellent and a net hood, which kept me sane. Otherwise I'm sure I'd have been driven crazy. Still, as I would discover over the next few days, dozens of the insects penetrated my defenses.

Nearly as troublesome, but a lot more fun, was a red squirrel that lived near the lean-to. Absolutely fearless, it was determined to explore my food bag. It would come to within two feet of me and start scratching at the bag— eyeing me all the while with something akin to defiant contempt. I poked at it with my walking stick, and it swatted at the end of it, like a cat. Finally it retreated a few feet, sat on its haunches, squeezed its eyes shut, clenched its fists, and chittered angrily at the sky, like a child throwing a tantrum.

After eating, I got out my trail guide to check on the next day's hike. Alone among the clubs the Maine Appalachian Trail Club prints detailed trail data on the backs of A.T. maps instead of in the bound guidebook, a nice innovation. I would have, I found, a hike the next day of 6.8 miles to Chairback Gap Lean-to. I would climb Fourth, Third, and Columbus Mountains, cross an "interesting bog, replete with pitcher plants," and pass, at mile 4.4, a blue-blazed side trail leading a hundred yards to a ledge with views south toward Indian Pond and Benson Mountain.

There are ten of these A.T. guidebooks, and they cover the trail in astounding detail. Guides to some of the hiking trails in the White Mountains appeared as far back as the last century. Guides to the A.T. itself first appeared in the 1930s. There was no standardization; local clubs put out any sort of guide they chose. Some clubs described the trail to a hundredth of a mile. In 1968 the Keystone Trails Association, in Pennsylvania, began covering the trail only to one-tenth of a mile and started putting the distances in the margins for easy reference. Now guidebooks are thoroughly revised every two to three years, generally, and most take several months to produce. The detail is still amazing.

Unexpected nuggets can be mined from the guides. The Maine guidebook warns, "Never warm a frozen foot or hand over an open fire—this cooks the flesh." Check.

In our litigious society the question of liability has arisen even in connection with the trail guidebooks. For instance, does a guide's mention of a spring imply that the water in the spring is safe for drinking? And can a hiker made ill by the water then hold the ATC or the Park Service responsible? Fearing liability suits, a number of states have recently begun removing pipes from springs along the trail, lest the pipes imply the water is potable. "Official vandalism," I heard a hiker call this.

A few years ago a woman bitten by a snake in a Maryland state park brought suit against the state for not adequately warning her about snakes. So most of the guidebooks now include an up-front disclaimer, disavowing responsibility for anything bad that might happen to a hiker on the trail, as well as a brief note about snakes. This one from a Virginia guide is typical: "Poisonous snakes (rattlesnakes and copperheads) may be encountered along the Trail. Hikers should study the most current recommended methods for treating snakebites before hiking."

But poisonous snakes are not a concern along the A.T. in Maine. Nor were mosquitoes and blackflies the next day of my hike, for it turned cold and rainy. By 10 a.m. the horizon was a uniform gray, and the rain had settled into a dismal pattern that was clearly going to last awhile. Boulders and rocks turned slippery, and tree roots were treacherous. Despite my poncho I was soon wet and cold. Up and down across the mountains I slowly trudged, scrambling over boulders and around fallen trees.

About midday I met Jeff McDowell and his dog, Bear. They had started at Katahdin and were heading south. Part coyote, part Australian sheepdog, Bear was carrying small saddlebags full of dog food. She was drenched, and stood, wet and bedraggled, while we talked. She looked like I felt.

When I began to think I must surely be getting close to the lean-to, I came to a signboard that said I had another 3.2 miles to go. In the afternoon the rain picked up, and the temperature fell. I sloshed through boggy areas, reminding myself that mud is just dust waiting its turn. My boots could not have been any wetter had I been wading streams; I squished with every step. To keep a change of clothes dry in my pack, I continued hiking in wet shorts and shirt, beneath a poncho. (Continued on page 184)

PAPER BIRCH *(Betula papyrifera)*

*Where an inch can make a difference,
backpacker Noel Grove squeezes through a
narrow crack in Mahoosuc Notch.
This mile of trail, considered by many
the A.T.'s most difficult, calls for giant steps
and steady nerves (opposite) in
an obstacle course created over millennia by
boulders tumbling from Mahoosuc
and Fulling Mill Mountains.*

*FOLLOWING PAGES: With autumn in the
air, a Maine couple fishes Moxie Pond. Recently
rerouted off a gravel road here, the A.T.
now cuts through woods on higher ground.*

*Heavy-laden hiker Tom Mullin
fords Baker Stream a short distance
from Moxie Pond; Roger the dog
seems to be having second
thoughts. The waterways and bogs of
Maine delight hikers but also
present a drawback: frequent damp feet.
False hellebore (below), also
known as Indian poke and devil's-bite,
thrives in such low, wet areas. Indians
used its powerful but poisonous
root medicinally, to slow the heartbeat
and to lower blood pressure.*

*Haven for trekkers, Shaw's
Boarding Home welcomes hikers to
Monson. Keith Shaw (left) and
his wife, Pat, put up some 600 visitors
a year, mostly A.T. hikers.
An all-you-can-eat
breakfast (above) includes eggs,
pancakes, sausage, hash browns,
doughnuts, juice, and
coffee. The price: $3.50. Northbound
hikers use Monson as their
last resupply point before setting off
for Katahdin, 116 miles away.*

Great blue heron, poised to fish in the quiet shallows
of Lake Hebron, outside Monson, stands in early
morning mist. The big birds frequently nest in dead trees near
lakes and ponds. Moose, often seen from the A.T.
in Maine, feed among the willows and
scrub of the well-watered forest or wade in shallow lakes,
browsing on aquatic plants. Frequently
they leave their cloven footprints on the trail.

*Revisiting scenes of his youth, Raymond Waugh
rest with his wife, Alice, during a hike
in Gulf Hagas, a chasm of slate cliffs along
the West Branch of the Pleasant River (right). As
a young man in the CCC, Ray worked
on clearing a section of the A.T. near here; this was
his first trip back in more than 50 years. Tumbled
boulders in the gorge shelter a diversity
of creatures, such as the garter snake below.*

Raft of autumn's
splendor—white pine needles,
along with leaves of white cedar,
poplar, birch,
maple—floats in the
water in Gulf Hagas. Below,
a fly agaric rises from the
forest floor. Milk
containing the cap of
this mushroom will stun or
even kill flies;
hence, its name.

FOLLOWING PAGES: Rushing
water and a shaded
shelter lure hikers to this
peaceful retreat on
Maine's Rainbow Stream.

(Continued from page 167) I thought Jeff had told me, when we chatted earlier, "Cross Third Mountain, and there's the shelter." But I crossed Third Mountain, and there was no shelter. I stopped and got out my map and found I had another mountain—Columbus—yet to cross. O woe!

My right knee began to feel funny.

It was late afternoon when I finally reached Chairback Gap Lean-to. I was soaked through and shivering with the cold, so—after forcing myself to make a trip, another 200 yards, to the spring for water—I got into all my dry clothing and then into my sleeping bag. I fired up my stove and fixed a cup of coffee. I cradled it in my hands, and the heat felt wonderful. I boiled more water for my freeze-dried supper—chicken and noodles—and could feel the warmth spreading through me as I ate. The rain continued to fall.

The sleeping bag I had brought was summer weight and turned out to be a little light for spring in Maine. So I lay awake a good part of the night, shivering, trying to scratch blackfly bites through three layers of clothing, and listening to a mouse gnawing on something in my pack.

If it's raining tomorrow, I vowed, I'm taking the day off.

It was raining.

It had rained through the night, the patter on the roof sometimes heavy. When morning came, the horizon was still gray and solid. It was colder; I lay in my sleeping bag and watched my breath rise toward the ceiling.

I was a little sorry I didn't have someone to share my discomfort with. Depending on your temperament, solo hiking can be one of life's great pleasures or an exercise in loneliness and boredom. Most people enjoy being on their own for a while but crave company, too. Even thru-hikers, asked why they hike, will often mention the solitude, but asked what they remember most from their hike, will rattle off the names and personalities of friends they made on the trail.

People seeking hiking partners look first among their families and friends, naturally, but failing there they advertise in the *Appalachian Trailway News.* It's a tricky proposition, finding a compatible companion among strangers, for hiking with someone is a little like being married: The stresses are unexpectedly severe. In 1985 the *Trailway News* surveyed the people who had advertised for partners to find out how successful they had been. Generally about half the respondents were able to locate and at least begin a hike with someone. But more than half of these failed to finish their hike together. The distances they managed to accomplish ranged from as little as 10 miles to as much as 900 miles. For some the breakup came after just two days.

Injury and illness were cited as the primary reasons for the splits. Asked if they would be willing to hike again with their same partners, only one gave an emphatic "No!" One thoughtful hiker wrote that finding a partner, if only for a little while, could ". . . help ease people into a thru-hike by removing their fears of being alone and lost in the wilderness."

Alone in the wilderness. . . .

NORTHERN RED OAK *(Quercus rubra)*

I made the best of my day off, watching juncos hop through the drizzle, eyeing the horizon for signs of clearer skies, tormenting another red squirrel. Occasional gusts of cold wind sent cloudlets of mist swirling into the shelter. I turned my back and hunched my shoulders. I made endless cups of coffee. My stove began acting up from the cold, so I brought the can of propane into my sleeping bag with me to warm it up. I read an old *Reader's Digest* someone had left at the shelter—"The Bugs That Bug Us: What You Should Know About Colds"—and pored over my maps, a perpetual source of interest. I used a dry pair of socks as gloves and got out of my sleeping bag only a couple of times—to make another trip to the spring and to warm up with some jumping jacks. Now and then a scraggly patch of blue sky would appear overhead, raising my spirits and my hopes. But still the rain came down.

And I thought about the A.T. and the people who use it.

What are we to make of this trail, finally, this ribbon of American mountains and valleys devoted to the simple pleasure of walking? It has grown from the vague imaginings of a handful of people to a mammoth enterprise, officially chartered and bylawed, that engages the devotion of thousands of volunteers. It is used by millions of people each year: some for a stroll of a few hours, some for brief weekend or week-long camping trips, some for weeks—or even months—of rigorous outdoor living. It has been debated in the halls of Congress, has survived the scrutiny and interest of state and federal bureaucrats, and has been found deserving of funding and protection.

Although much progress has been made since 1972, the A.T. is *not* protected yet. There will probably be corridor violations—theft of timber, for instance—to contend with. The Forest Service, pressured by a financially strapped federal government to produce more revenue, continues to lace the woodlands with roads, bringing noise, dust, vandalism, and litter deeper into its remote forests. The cumulative impact of these road networks near the A.T. can change the character of the trail environment. But according to Dave Sherman: "The most serious threat to the trail is the rapidly increasing development that approaches the corridor. If our senators and representatives suddenly ceased funding the protection effort, we would be hard-pressed to save the trail. So much of the A.T.'s value depends on the illusion or sense of remoteness; hence, it is critical to buffer the trail from visual intrusions by a corridor of adequate width." Lands critically needed for this narrow, fragile corridor still remain to be acquired by the Forest and Park Services. Only the continued commitment of both houses of Congress will ensure that the entire trail will be passed on to new generations of hikers.

And how about A.T. hikers? What are we to make of them? As tough as woodpeckers, as shy as deer, as independent as cats, and as gaudy—with their green, blue, and red backpacks—as parrots, they wander through the mountains, appearing on the trail as mysteriously as puffs of mist, then as quietly and inexplicably wafting onward. They suffer discomfort gladly but are outraged by the sound of a chain saw. They live for weeks on gorp and peanut butter, dreaming of milk shakes and prime rib. They climb endless mountains, as laden as mules, for views they would ignore from the window of an airplane. Forever restless and eager to be hitting the trail, they can sit and stare into a campfire for hours without moving. They have the charm of

185

chipmunks and the courage of squirrels. Generally a peaceable and gentle bunch, they are for the most part worthy of the trail they so admire.

Just at sunset the rain finally stopped, and the sky began to clear. A fierce wind arose and blew far into the night. The next day promised to be a pretty one, so I was up and packed and on my way early. Moose tracks appeared in the mud of the trail, and birds flitted through treetops. About time my luck changed, I thought. Mosquitoes, blackflies, cold, rain—that's enough for one trip. Then my luck gave out altogether.

Bouncing along down an easy stretch of trail, I stepped on the edge of a slippery rock, my ankle turned, and I pitched forward onto my face. My 40-pound pack landed on the back of my head. It was like being hit from behind by a pickup.

I wiggled and squirmed for a minute, like a bug on its back, before I could get myself upright again. The sprain was pretty bad, I could tell, bad enough anyway to put a stop to a hike.

I gathered myself up and hobbled a couple of miles to a gravel logging road. I was seven miles from civilization and set off gamely in that direction—but couldn't do it. I sat down on my pack alongside the road and waited. When an enormous truck came along, I flagged it down: cloud of dust, hissing brakes, tons of logs rocking back and forth, a jolly driver grinning down at me from his cab high overhead. He took me to a telephone, and by nightfall I was scrubbed and taped and dining on steak and baked potato—"Would you pass the butter, please"—back at Shaw's, in Monson.

The lesson is plain. Sometimes it's better just to hang up your pack and come back to hike another day. Sometimes the elements will conspire to topple your carefully laid plans and turn your hike into a catalog of miseries. But sometimes everything goes right.

And that's the way I finished the trail last year. At the base finally of Katahdin, the tallest mountain in Maine, I had caught up with the elusive Jerry Gramling, the young hiker whose parents Sam and I had met in Georgia and whose progress I had been tracking for months. At Daicey Pond Campground I had queried three thru-hikers about him.

"Do you know Jerry Gramling?" I asked.

"Yes," said one. "Tall kid with a beard. Quiet."

"Real quiet," said another.

"*Very* quiet," said the third.

I knew his mother and father had been planning to come to Maine to climb Katahdin with him, and I found the whole family at a campground outside Baxter State Park. Father and son were soaking in a Jacuzzi, and Mrs. Gramling was cooking supper in their cabin.

Over sloppy joes, we got Jerry to reminisce a bit about his incredible 2,100-mile walk. About the early cold in the South: "I had snow until Hot Springs." About animals: "I was too early for bears in the Smokies, but I saw some in the Shenandoahs. A moose watched me ford the Kennebec." About food: "I lost around 20 pounds." About his future: "Probably college, for a degree in business."

The next day dawned clear and cool. The ranger at Katahdin Stream Campground said there were usually just three or four such perfect days in a

186

hiking season. I was on the trail early, for the climb of Katahdin, the "greatest mountain" of the Abenaki Indians, can be a full day's work. It's five steep miles up to its 5,267-foot summit, then those same five steep miles back down again. Middle-aged knees can feel the strain.

You climb first through mostly beeches, birches, and maples. You cross Katahdin Stream and climb some more with a noisy waterfall on the left. The forest, increasingly dominated by conifers, gets smaller as you begin the steep part. Spruce and fir trees shrink to bush size, then peter out altogether. At timberline you ascend even more steeply through huge boulders. A few have iron rungs hammered into them for handholds.

About a quarter of the way up Jerry passed me, moving fast; his parents were somewhere behind, giving it a try.

At the Gateway things began to level off. The sky was still a cloudless blue, and much of Maine seemed to be spread at my feet. The wind was howling. Tiny icicles on the rocks pointed in the direction the wind was blowing and dripped in the sunshine. I crossed a mile of the Tableland, its rocks covered with pale green and rust-colored lichens, then climbed the last ridge to the plaques and signboards of the summit. I could barely stand directly on the peak, so fierce was the wind, but a few feet down one way or the other the boulders offered quiet shelter.

I found quite a crowd at the summit. One of the thru-hikers, a young man from Canada, was celebrating a birthday, and a dozen or so of his fellow hikers had arranged to finish their hikes with him on the same day. They were a giddy bunch, laughing and exuberant, shaking hands and hugging one another, passing around cameras and posing for photos, sharing treats from a final lunch. A small gray mouse—an astonishingly hardy little creature—came out from its nest among the boulders and begged for crackers.

It's almost impossible to imagine the exhilaration thru-hikers must feel, after months of the most strenuous toil, to finally reach this spot: "O be swift, my soul, to answer Him! be jubilant my feet. . . ." I looked around for Jerry, and my final image of him seems appropriate: Here, at the very end of the Appalachian Trail, he was sitting a little apart from the others, hugging his knees in the cold, staring north across miles of lakes and forests toward the unending and trackless wilderness of Canada. ☐

BUNCHBERRY *(Cornus canadensis)*

End in sight:
At Daicey Pond,
hiker Ben Brantley faces
just seven more miles
to Katahdin,
here reflected in the
water. In an
average year
some 100 thru-hikers
walk all 2,100 miles of
the A.T. Others
become "2,000-milers,"
completing the
trail after several years of
hiking segments of it.

*Final strenuous climb takes hikers to the crown of
Katahdin, centerpiece of Baxter State Park.
Thru-hikers Albie Pokrob and Linwood Gill (below) assess the
remaining miles, and Sugar and Dawson Wheeler (right)
stop for lunch on the Tableland. At the summit
Linwood prepares a victory sandwich of peanut butter and
M&Ms. In 1930 former governor Percival Baxter began acquiring land
in the northern Maine wilderness and donating
it to the state. Today his gift of more than 200,000 acres
honors his vision of "forever wild" parkland.*

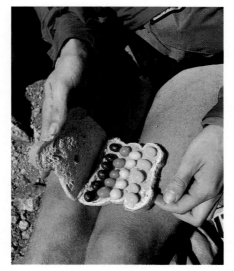

*Fog bathes the summit of Katahdin
as the Wheelers near the top.
The Tennessee couple
spent six months honeymooning
on the trail. Hand in hand
(above) they approach the signboard
at the 5,267-foot peak, where
the white paint blazes end.*

*FOLLOWING PAGES: On top of
the world a hiker on Katahdin has
Maine at her feet. Reaching
the summit, hikers exult in their
accomplishment and
praise the path that brought them
here—the Appalachian Trail.*

ACKNOWLEDGMENTS

The Special Publications Division is especially grateful for the assistance of David M. Sherman, Office of Land Use, National Park Service; Brian B. King, Director of Public Affairs, Appalachian Trail Conference; Charles R. Rinaldi, Project Manager, National Park Service Appalachian Trail Project Office; Paul Brewster, Resource Management Specialist, U.S. Forest Service, on assignment to the N.P.S. Appalachian Trail Project Office; and Theodore R. Dudley, Research Botanist, U.S. National Arboretum. We would also like to thank the Appalachian Trail Conference, the National Park Service, the U.S. Forest Service, the Potomac Appalachian Trail Club, the individuals and organizations named or quoted in the text, and those cited here for their generous assistance: Richard Ackerman, Bill Adams, Fred J. Alsop III, John Barbour, Anne Bennett, Warren Bielenberg, Thomas Birch, Kenneth E. Bisbee, Charles A. Blankenship, Kirby A. Brock, Richard C. Bruce, Sandy Campbell, Dennis Carter, V. Collins Chew, Terry Chilcoat, Larry Collins, Joseph F. Cook, Bjorn Dahl, Jane and Walter Daniels, Kim Delozier, Richard Donahoe, A. Murray Evans, David B. Field, Jack Focht, Maurice J. Forrester, Jr., Marc Fortin, Dennis Frye, Don Hale, Steve Hendricks, Dave Hinchen, Jean Hoekwater, Chester Jenkins, Peter Jensen, Earl Jette, Kenneth D. Kimball, Donald T. King, Scott F. Larcher, Keith Lawrence, Elizabeth D. Levers, Karen L. Lutz, Thomas Margiotta, Burnham Martin, Jean McAlister, Bruce McFate, Orson K. Miller, Jr., John M. Morgan, James Nelson, Norm Peachey, Harry T. Peet, Jr., Kevin Peterson, Robert W. Poole, James R. Preston, Reuben Rajala, Marilyn and Ron Rosen, William E. Rosevear, Clebe W. Scott, Stanley E. Senner, Nancy Shofner, Bob Slack, Morgan Sommerville, Ken Spalding, Richard Strattan, Edith L. Sweigert, Edward N. Therrien, Michael Torrey, Charles Trivett, Jim Vincent, Laura and Guy Waterman, Douglas H. West, J. Peter Wilshusen, Cynthia L. Wright, Thomas E. Wright, Jr.

For statistical information on New England forests we are indebted to Mollie Beattie, et al., *Working with Your Woodland: A Landowner's Guide* (Hanover, New Hampshire: The University Press of New England, 1983).

For quotations from hymns we gratefully acknowledge the following: C. A. Bowen, ed., *The Cokesbury Worship Hymnal* (New York: The Methodist Publishing House, 1938); Homer A. Rodeheaver, compiler, *Victory Songs* (Chicago and Philadelphia: The Rodeheaver Company, n.d.).

Stuffed with necessities and decked with creature comforts, a backpack tells a story of the toils of a lone hiker's life on the trail.

Composition for this book by the Typographic section of National Geographic Production Services, Pre-Press Division. Printed and bound by Holladay-Tyler Printing Corp., Glenn Dale, Md. Film preparation by Catharine Cooke Studio, Inc., New York, N.Y. Color separations by Lanman Progressive Company, Washington, D.C.; Lincoln Graphics, Inc., Cherry Hill, N.J.; and NEC, Inc., Nashville, Tenn. Dust jacket printed by Federated Lithographers-Printers, Inc., Providence, R.I.

Library of Congress CIP Data
Fisher, Ronald M.
    Mountain adventure : exploring the Appalachian Trail / by Ronald M. Fisher ; photographed by Sam Abell ; prepared by the Special Publications Division, National Geographic Society.
        p.   cm.
    Includes index.
    ISBN 0-87044-668-1 (regular edition)
    ISBN 0-87044-673-8 (library edition)
    1. Hiking—Appalachian Trail. 2. Appalachian Trail—Description and travel. 3. Appalachian Trail—History. 4. Natural history—Appalachian Trail. I. Abell, Sam. II. National Geographic Society (U. S.). Special Publications Division. III. Title.
GV199.42.A68F47 1988
917.4—dc19   88-29053
                                                      CIP

Index

Boldface indicates illustrations;
italic refers to picture captions.

198

ADDITIONAL READING AND INFORMATION

Readers may wish to consult the *National Geographic Index* for related books and articles. The following may also prove useful: Maurice Graham Brooks, *The Appalachians;* V. Collins Chew, *Underfoot: A Geologic Guide to the A.T.;* Thomas L. Connelly, *Discovering the Appalachians;* James M. and Hertha E. Flack, *Ambling and Scrambling on the Appalachian Trail;* Colin Fletcher, *The Complete Walker III: The Joys and Techniques of Hiking and Backpacking;* Michael Frome, *Strangers in High Places: The Story of the Great Smoky Mountains;* Edward B. Garvey, *Appalachian Hiker* and *Appalachian Hiker II;* James R. Hare, ed., *Hiking the Appalachian Trail;* Frederick W. Kilbourne, *Chronicles of the White Mountains;* Sandra Kocher and Michael Warren, *Appalachian Trail;* Charlton Ogburn, *The Southern Appalachians: A Wilderness Quest;* Robert J. Redington, *Survey of the Appalachians;* Earl V. Shaffer, *Walking with Spring;* Ann and Myron Sutton, *The Appalachian Trail: Wilderness on the Doorstep.*

The various publications of the Appalachian Trail Conference are valuable sources of information for those considering hiking all or part of the Appalachian Trail. These include the ten volumes of trail guides, the newsletters *Appalachian Trailway News* and *The Register,* and annually updated versions of *The Appalachian Trail Data Book.* For more information contact the Appalachian Trail Conference, P.O. Box 807, Harpers Ferry, West Virginia 25425-0807. Telephone: (304) 535-6331.

NATIONAL GEOGRAPHIC SOCIETY

"For the increase and diffusion of geographic knowledge"

THE NATIONAL GEOGRAPHIC SOCIETY is chartered in Washington, D. C., as a nonprofit scientific and educational organization. Since 1890 the Society has supported more than 3,400 explorations and research projects, adding to knowledge of earth, sea, and sky.

GILBERT M. GROSVENOR, *President*
OWEN R. ANDERSON, *Executive Vice President*
ALFRED J. HAYRE, *Vice President and Treasurer*
Vice Presidents:
FREDERICK C. GALE, LEONARD J. GRANT, JOSEPH B. HOGAN, JAMES P. KELLY, ADRIAN L. LOFTIN, JR., LEWIS P. LOWE, RAYMOND T. McELLIGOTT, JR., ROSS L. MULFORD, CLETIS PRIDE
ROBERT B. SIMS, *Communications*
EDWIN W. SNIDER, *Secretary*
SUZANNE DUPRÉ, *Corporate Counsel*

BOARD OF TRUSTEES

GILBERT M. GROSVENOR, *Chairman*
OWEN R. ANDERSON, *Vice Chairman*
LLOYD H. ELLIOTT, *Vice Chairman*
President, National Geographic Education Foundation
Chairmen Emeritus:
MELVIN M. PAYNE, THOMAS W. McKNEW
JOE L. ALLBRITTON
Chairman, Riggs National Bank
THOMAS E. BOLGER
Chairman of the Board, Bell Atlantic
FRANK BORMAN
Vice Chairman, Texas Air Corporation
LEWIS M. BRANSCOMB
Kennedy School of Government, Harvard University
ROBERT L. BREEDEN
J. CARTER BROWN
Director, National Gallery of Art
WARREN E. BURGER
Chief Justice of the United States (Ret.)
MICHAEL COLLINS
President, Michael Collins Associates
GEORGE M. ELSEY
President Emeritus, American Red Cross
WILBUR E. GARRETT
ARTHUR B. HANSON, Counsel Emeritus
ALFRED J. HAYRE
A. LEON HIGGINBOTHAM, JR.
U. S. Court of Appeals, Third Circuit
CARLISLE H. HUMELSINE, Chairman,
Executive Committee, Smithsonian Institution Regents
JOHN JAY ISELIN
President, The Cooper Union
J. WILLARD MARRIOTT, JR.
Chairman and President, Marriott Corporation
FLORETTA DUKES McKENZIE
Former Superintendent of Schools, District of Columbia
NATHANIEL P. REED
Businessman-Environmentalist
B. FRANCIS SAUL II
President, B. F. Saul Company
ROBERT C. SEAMANS, JR.
Department of Aeronautics and Astronautics, MIT

TRUSTEES EMERITUS

CRAWFORD H. GREENEWALT, CARYL P. HASKINS, MRS. LYNDON B. JOHNSON, CURTIS E. LEMAY, WM. McCHESNEY MARTIN, JR., LAURANCE S. ROCKEFELLER, FREDERICK G. VOSBURGH, JAMES H. WAKELIN, JR., JAMES E. WEBB, CONRAD L. WIRTH

COMMITTEE FOR RESEARCH AND EXPLORATION

MELVIN M. PAYNE, *Chairman;* T. DALE STEWART, BARRY C. BISHOP, *Vice Chairmen;* HARM J. DE BLIJ, *Editor, National Geographic Research;* EDWIN W. SNIDER, *Secretary;* WILBUR E. GARRETT, GILBERT M. GROSVENOR, CARYL P. HASKINS, THOMAS W. McKNEW, BETTY J. MEGGERS, Research Associate-Anthropology, Smithsonian Institution, PETER H. RAVEN, Director, Missouri Botanical Garden, CHARLES H. SOUTHWICK, Professor of Biology, University of Colorado, JOHN H. STEELE, Director, Woods Hole Oceanographic Institution, GEORGE E. STUART, JAMES H. WAKELIN, JR., GEORGE E. WATSON, FRANK C. WHITMORE, JR., Research Geologist, U. S. Geological Survey, HENRY T. WRIGHT, Professor of Anthropology, University of Michigan

NATIONAL GEOGRAPHIC MAGAZINE

GILBERT M. GROSVENOR, *President and Chairman* **WILBUR E. GARRETT,** *Editor*
JOSEPH JUDGE, *Senior Associate Editor* **THOMAS R. SMITH,** *Associate Editor*
CHARLES McCARRY, *Editor-at-Large*

SENIOR ASSISTANT EDITORS

THOMAS Y. CANBY, *Science* JOHN B. GARVER, Jr., *Cartography* WILLIAM GRAVES, *Expeditions*
THOMAS R. KENNEDY, *Photography* ROBERT W. MADDEN, *Layout* SAMUEL W. MATTHEWS, *Production*
O. LOUIS MAZZATENTA, *Control Center* BART McDOWELL, *Contract Writers*
ELIZABETH A. MOIZE, *Legends* HOWARD E. PAINE, *Art* JOHN J. PUTMAN, *Manuscripts*
LESLEY B. ROGERS, *Research* W. ALLAN ROYCE, *Illustrations*
MARY G. SMITH, *Research Grant Projects* GERARD A. VALERIO, *Design*

EDITORIAL

ASSISTANT EDITORS: William S. Ellis, Rowe Findley, Rick Gore, Alice J. Hall, Merle Severy, Peter T. White. **SENIOR WRITERS:** Thomas J. Abercrombie, Harvey Arden, David S. Boyer, Mike Edwards, Noel Grove, Bryan Hodgson, Michael E. Long, Priit J. Vesilind. **SENIOR EDITORIAL STAFF:** Robert Booth, Judith Brown, John L. Eliot, Boyd Gibbons, David Jeffery, Larry Kohl, Douglas B. Lee, Peter Miller, Cathy Newman, Cliff Tarpy, Jane Vessels. *Production:* John L. McIntosh. **EDITORIAL STAFF:** Don Belt, Charles E. Cobb, Jr., Louise E. Levathes, Boris Weintraub. **RESEARCH:** Michaeline A. Sweeney, *Assoc. Director; Researcher-Editors:* Carolyn H. Anderson, Ann B. Henry, Jeanne E. Peters. *Researchers:* Danielle M. Beauchamp, Catherine C. Fox, Jan Holderness, Anne A. Jamison, Amy E. Kezerian, Kathy B. Maher, Barbara W. McConnell, Jean B. McConville, Miriam R. Miller, Abigail A. Tipton, Margaret N. Walsh, Cheryl Weissman. *Legends:* Victoria C. Ducheneaux. *Planning Council:* Jan Hambling, Mary McPeak

ILLUSTRATIONS

PHOTOGRAPHERS: Kent J. Kobersteen, *Asst. Director;* James L. Amos, Joseph H. Bailey, James P. Blair, Victor R. Boswell, Jr., Jodi Cobb, Bruce Dale, Emory Kristof, Joseph D. Lavenburg, Bates Littlehales, George F. Mobley, Steve Raymer, James L. Stanfield; *Admin.:* Susan A. Smith, Alvin M. Chandler, Claude E. Petrone, Maria Stenzel. **ILLUSTRATIONS EDITORS:** Robert W. Hernandez, *Asst. Director;* William L. Allen, David L. Arnold, William T. Douthitt, Bruce A. McElfresh, Charlene Murphy, Robert S. Patton, Elie S. Rogers, Jon Schneeberger, Susan Welchman. **LAYOUT:** Constance H. Phelps, *Asst. Dir.* **DESIGN:** Betty Clayman-DeAtley, *Asst. Dir.;* Timothy J. Conroy, Douglas M. McKenney. **ART:** Jan Adkins, J. Robert Teringo, Charles C. Uhl, *Assoc. Dirs.;* Allen Carroll, *Asst. Dir.; Artist:* William H. Bond. *Research:* Karen E. Gibbs. **ENGRAVING AND PRINTING:** William W. Smith, *Director;* James R. Whitney, *Assoc. Dir.;* Judy L. Garvey, John W. Gergel, Ronald E. Williamson

CARTOGRAPHY

Assoc. Directors: Harold E. Aber, Jr., John F. Shupe; *Sr. Asst. Dir.:* Alice T. M. Rechlin; *Asst. Dirs.:* David P. Beddoe, John F. Dorr, Harold A. Hanson, Harry D. Kauhane, Richard K. Rogers, Elie Sabban, Leo B. Zebarth. *Archaeologist:* George E. Stuart. *Geographer:* Ted Dachtera. *Map Editors:* Charles W. Gotthardt, Jr., *Supvr.;* John T. Blozis, Thomas L. Gray, Etelka K. Horvath, Gus Platis, Jon A. Sayre, Thomas A. Wall, Thomas A. Walsh. *Designers:* Lisa Biganzoli, John A. Bonner, Nancy Schweickart, Sally Suominen-Summerall. *Researchers:* Dorothy A. Nicholson, *Supvr.;* John L. Beeson, Dierdre T. Bevington, Ross M. Emerson, Marguerite B. Hunsiker, Linda R. Kriete, Gaither G. Kyhos, Mary C. Latham, David B. Miller, Douglas A. Strobel, Juan J. Valdés, Andrew J. Wahll, Susan Young. *Text:* Oliver G.A.M. Payne. *Map Artists:* Roland R. Nichols, *Supvr.;* Iskandar Baday, James E. McClelland, Jr., Stephen P. Wells, Alfred L. Zebarth. *Computer Cartography:* Timothy J. Carter, Charles F. Case, Arthur J. Cox, Martin J. Golden. *Specialists:* Charles L. Miller, Henri A. Delanghe, Edward J. Holland

EDITORIAL SERVICES

ADMINISTRATION: M. Jean Vile, Benita M. Swash, *Assts. to the Editor;* Elaine Rice Ames, Marie L. Barnes, Mary L. Blanton, Marisa Domeyko, Neva L. Folk, Lilian Davidson, Virginia H. Finnegan, Eleanor W. Hahne, Ellen E. Kohlberg, Karen S. Marsh, Liisa Maurer, Katherine P. McGown, Susan S. Norton, Carol D. Rhoads, Emmy Scammahorn, Charlene S. Valeri. *Picture Requests:* Barbara A. Shattuck. *Correspondence:* Carolyn F. Clewell, Joseph M. Blanton, Jr. *Indexes:* Jolene M. Blozis, Anne K. McCain. *Travel:* Virginia A. Bachant, Ann C. Judge. **LIBRARIES:** *Publications:* Susan Fifer Canby, *Director;* Patricia Murphy Smith, Arlene T. Drewes, Carolyn Locke, Marta Strada. *Records & Illustrations:* Lorie Northrop, *Director;* L. Fern Dame, Mary Anne McMillen, Carolyn J. Harrison, Ann E. Hubbs, Maura A. Mulvihill, Mennen M. Smith. **NEWS SERVICE:** Paul Sampson, *Director;* Joy Aschenbach, Mercer Cross, Kenneth C. Danforth, Donald J. Frederick, Barbara S. Moffet. *Radio:* Robert C. Radcliffe. **AUDIOVISUAL:** Joanne M. Hess, *Director;* Jon H. Larimore, *Tech. Dir.;* Dean Conger, *Multi-image Dir.;* Ronald S. Altemus, Robert G. Fleegal, Paul Gorski, P. Andrew van Duym, Gerald L. Wiley

ADMINISTRATION

ASST. VICE PRESIDENTS: Joyce W. Graves, *Asst. to the President;* Robert G. Corey, Thomas E. Kulikosky, Carol E. Lang, H. Gregory Platts, Carl M. Shrader, Paul B. Tylor. **ASST. TREASURER:** Dorothy M. Wagner. **GEOGRAPHIC LIAISON:** Barry C. Bishop. **ASSTS. TO THE PRESIDENT:** Richard E. Pearson, *Diplomatic and Civic Affairs;* Robert E. Dulli, *Education.* **ACCOUNTING:** Dorothy J. Edwards, Douglas E. Hill, Laura L. Leight, George E. Newstedt. **ADMINISTRATION:** D. Evelyn Carnahan, Margaret R. Herndon, Robert V. Koenig, Zbigniew Jan Lutyk, Marta M. Marschalko, Myra A. McLellan, Jennifer Moseley, Shirley Neff, Janet C. Newell, Jimmie D. Pridemore, Joyce S. Sanford, Myla Stewart, Frank M. Twigger. **COMPUTER:** Scott Bolden, Warren Burger, William L. Chewning, George F. Hubbs, Ronald C. Kline, Richard A. Mechler, James G. Schmelzer, Harold E. Smith. **EDUCATIONAL SERVICES:** Wendy G. Rogers, Dean R. Gage, Carl W. Harmon, Jr., Albert Meyer. **MEMBERSHIP SERVICES:** Margaret L. Bassford, Robert C. Dove, Carol A. Houck, Marguerite M. Wise, Peter F. Woods. **PERSONNEL:** Robert E. Howell, Glenn G. Pepperman, Shirley N. Wilson. **PROMOTION:** Joseph S. Fowler, Joan Anderson, James R. Dimond, Jr., Robert L. Feige, Deborah A. Jones, Charles T. Kneeland, Lucy J. Lowenthal, F. William Rath. **PURCHASING:** Margaret Cole, Thomas L. Fletcher

PRODUCTION SERVICES

QUALITY: Frank S. Oliverio, Bill M. Aldridge. **PRE-PRESS:** Geoffrey T. McConnell, Billy R. Barnett, Richard A. Bredeck, Ellwood M. Kohler, Jr., Phillip E. Plude, Bernard G. Quarrick. **PHOTOGRAPHIC LAB:** William S. Petrini, David H. Chisman, James H. Trott, Alfred M. Yee. **PRINTING:** Hans H. Wegner, Joseph M. Anderson, Sherrie S. Harrison. **ADMINISTRATION:** Lawrence F. Ludwig, *Director;* Joan S. Simms

ADVERTISING

George E. Moffat, *Vice President and Director.* Jack Lynch, *National Sales Manager-East.* Philip G. Reynolds, *National Sales Manager-West.* James D. Shepherd, *Western Regional Manager.* O. W. Jones, Jr., *Detroit Manager.* Robert D. Johnson, *Los Angeles Manager.* Michel A. Boutin, 90, Champs Élysées, 75008 Paris, *International Advertising Director. Washington, D. C.:* Pandora Browne, *Promotion.* G. Sarita Lapham, *Operations.* Alex MacRae, *Marketing/Sales.* Renee Schewe-Clepper, *Research.* Gail M. Jackson, *Production*

TELEVISION

Tim T. Kelly, *Vice President and Director;* Yeorgos N. Lampathakis, Marjorie M. Moomey, Nola L. Shrewsberry, Kathleen F. Teter

EDUCATIONAL SERVICES OF THE SOCIETY

ROBERT L. BREEDEN, *Senior Vice President*

Danforth P. Fales, *Vice President;* William R. Gray, *Exec. Asst.;* Suzanne J. Jacobson, *Asst. to the Sr. Vice Pres.;* Stephen J. Hubbard, Betsy Ellison. **BOOK SERVICE:** Charles O. Hyman, *Director and Sr. Asst. Editor;* Ross Bennett, *Assoc. Dir.;* David M. Seager, *Art Dir.;* Greta Arnold, Mary Dickinson, John T. Dunn, Susan C. Eckert, Karen F. Edwards, Charlotte Golin, J. Edward Lanouette, Carol B. Lutyk, Linda B. Meyerriecks, Elizabeth Newhouse, M. Patt-Corner, R. M. Poole, David F. Robinson, Margaret Sedeen, Penelope Timbers, Jonathan Tourtellot, Richard Wain. **SPECIAL PUBLICATIONS:** Donald J. Crump, *Director and Sr. Asst. Editor;* Philip B. Silcott, *Assoc. Dir.;* Bonnie S. Lawrence, *Asst. Dir.;* Jody Bolt, *Art Dir.;* John G. Agnone, Leslie Allen, Jane H. Buxton, Margery G. Dunn, Toni Eugene, David V. Evans, Ron Fisher, Patricia F. Frakes, Sallie M. Greenwood, Mary Ann Harrell, Charles E. Herron, Alice Jablonsky, Anne D. Kobor, Paul Martin, Jane R. McCauley, Tom Melham, Robert Messer, H. Robert Morrison, Thomas O'Neill, Barbara A. Payne, Thomas B. Powell III, Cynthia Ramsay, Cinda Rose, David V. Showers, Gene S. Stuart, Jennifer C. Urquhart, George V. White. **WORLD:** Pat Robbins, *Editor;* Margaret McKelway, *Assoc. Editor;* Ursula Vosseler, *Art Dir.;* Jacqueline Geschickter, Pat Holland, Veronica Morrison, Judith Rinard, Eleanor Shannahan. **EDUCATIONAL MEDIA:** George A. Peterson, *Director;* Jimmie Abercrombie, David Beacom, Monica P. Bradsher, James B. Caffrey, Betty G. Kotcher, Sandra L. Matthews, Louise C. Millikan. **TRAVELER:** Joan Tapper, *Editor;* David R. Bridge, *Illus. Dir.;* Suez B. Kehl, *Art Dir.* **PUBLICATIONS ART:** John D. Garst, Jr., *Director;* Virginia L. Baza, *Assoc. Dir.;* Isaac Ortiz, *Asst. Dir.;* Peter J. Balch. **EDUCATIONAL FILMS:** Sidney Platt, *Director;* Donald M. Cooper, *Assoc. Dir.;* Suzanne K. Poole, Carl E. Ziebe

NATIONAL GEOGRAPHIC magazine makes an ideal gift for any occasion. For information about membership in the National Geographic Society, call 800-638-4077, toll free, or write to the National Geographic Society, Dept. 1675, Washington, D. C. 20036.